Pepper Becoming

The Journey of an Unwanted Dog and the Man Who Wanted Her

By John D. Visconti, CPDT-KA
and Pepper M. Visconti, Good Dog

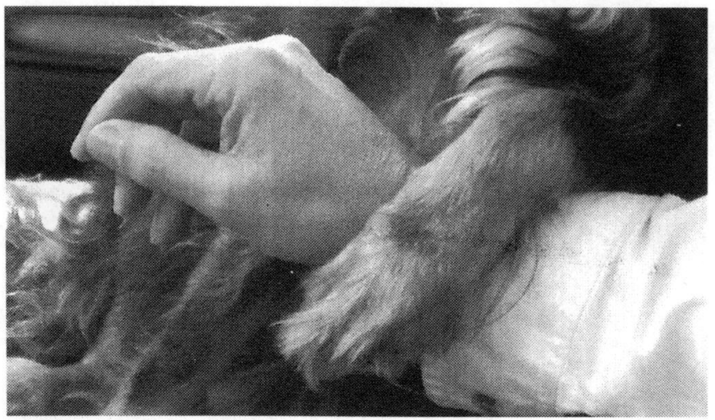

Pepper Becoming

John D. Visconti, CPDT-KA
www.pepperbecoming.com

Published by Rising Star Dog Services, LLC

Editor: Adrienne Hovey (www.freshstartwriting.com)
Cover Design: Dianne Paulet (www.dmpdesigns.com)
Internal Page Design: www.polgarusstudio.com

The names of some people and places in this book have been changed out of respect for the privacy of those involved in the story.

ISBN- 978-0-692-14530-2

Dedication: Hey Pepps. Woof.

Contents

The Opening Act

I'm not a big fan of book introductions. I can't tell you the last time (or first time) I made it through one. Book introductions are like a bad opening act at a concert. They are something to be endured while waiting for the main act to hit the stage.

That said, honestly, this introduction is necessary.

I'm also not a big fan of *thinking.* In fact, I rarely trust anything that emanates from my brain. Instead, I am instinctive and try not to define, label, or explain things unless it's absolutely necessary to do so. The best reaction to most situations is to follow Pepper's philosophy — say "Woof" and move on.

Despite those beliefs, rather than run the risk of not providing clarity for the reasons behind my actions recounted in the following pages, I will attempt to do so in order to avoid misinterpretation.

To begin with, I never intended to write a book about Pepper. Emails that appear throughout were only available because I'm too lazy to delete them from my accounts. I have emails dating back to 2007. Photographs in this book were the product of momentary inspiration: "Hey, I think I'll snap a picture of that." Nothing more. Nothing less. The same can be said for the videos cited at the end of the book.

Additionally, there is no underlying message, purpose, or agenda contained in the following pages. When writing, I simply sat quietly and listened to my heart while noting whatever I was feeling. It was like taking silent dictation.

This book tells the story of the years I spent caring for a wonderful yet troubled dog. During that time, I often made changes to my life — some would call them sacrifices — and devoted my time and energy — some would say quite a lot of both — working to help her overcome the behavioral challenges and fears she faced due to her difficult start in life. When she became ill, those changes, and that time and energy, multiplied immeasurably, and the physical and emotional toll on me was profound.

Some will read this story and wonder why I did what I did, and why I made the choices I made. Plain and simple, there were no *reasons* for anything I did. I was never once aware that I was doing something extraordinary (as noted by others), nor do I feel that now. I was just *doing.* The math was simple — it was easier to *do* than *not.* After reading this book, I suspect that many will walk away with an appreciation, maybe an astonishment, for what I did for Pepper. But truth be told, I never saw it that way. Pepper and I served a purpose in each other's lives. As far as what that purpose was — woof. With certainty I can say that I was partly motivated by self-interest. And I'm OK with that. Heck, even Gandhi said that "altruism and self-interest are both acceptable as reasons for action." It just felt good to help her. Why? Woof.

It is important to note that I don't look at how other people interact with or care for their dogs through the filter of my experiences with Pepper. I have enough to do just to keep myself afloat every day without investing precious time and energy being judgmental about the actions of others, except for those who are cruel to dogs. My situation with Pepper was exceptionally unique. To begin with, I'm a certified dog trainer. Where others see "problem" behaviors with their dogs, I see fascinating challenges. That's why I'm a trainer. Regarding my daily care of Pepper, especially toward the end of her life, I possessed the financial resources that allowed me to afford her care and to stay home with her. For that, I am blessed and eternally grateful. But it's not something everyone can do. And I'm also OK with that.

The way I figure, if I climbed Mount Everest, I wouldn't have anything negative to say about others who haven't. We all have our lives to lead.

~~~~~~

I have titled this book "Pepper Becoming" in recognition of the fact that through the years her story has continually evolved, even after she exited this planet.

Wise Zen words teach, "Nothing exists. All things are becoming." What exists in this moment changes in the next. Even historical events, such as those recounted in this book, have taken on new meaning since I began documenting the story of our shared journey.

During a horribly dark first five years of life, Pepper had been cast aside by nearly all who knew her. She struggled mightily to navigate a world that at times caused her debilitating anxiety. And despite a terribly arduous final 18 months, which she met with heroic grace, her spirit and zest for life never dampened. Every fetch ball was the best fetch ball ever. Every car ride was an incomparable adventure. Every puzzle game, tug-of-war, and Easter egg hunt were akin to a kid's first ride on a brand new, shiny bicycle. For Pepper, every good moment was the best moment ever.

Directly and indirectly she touched the lives of countless people and, even in her absence, continues to do so. She graced our lives with her presence during a colorfully eventful, loving, and sometimes challenging 8 ½ years.

And now, the lights dim, the crowd quiets, anticipation is in the air. Ladies and gentlemen…
~~~~~~

Full Cycle

He was old and scarecrow-thin. His face was timeworn and carried an expression suggesting that, while physically present, his thoughts were elsewhere. He appeared frail and unsteady, but determined, as he shuffled on a path at the Great Tails Animal Shelter. In his right hand, pressed against his chest he clutched a small bouquet of red and yellow flowers. The flowers struck a harmonious balance with this beautiful, warm, and peaceful Sunday morning — the type of morning that seemingly only occurs on Sundays.

Bathed in sunlight while sitting in the grass, Pepper and I observed as he slowly flickered from view, into the dense trees that lined the end of the narrow dirt path. When he was out of sight, we resumed our discussion about squirrels, treats, and how she'd soon be living with me. She expressed her approval by wrapping her right paw around my arm while I petted her chest. As I kissed her on the top of the head, I heard, "Yeah...she'll let you do that but no one else." The voice was that of a shelter worker who, along with two other employees, was arriving for her day's work. "She'll let you do it too," I responded as I motioned them over. "No thanks. We're afraid," was her reply, as the others nodded their heads in agreement.

I was beginning to understand how this dog, whom I considered pure gold, was still living in the shelter. She had not only been misunderstood but also demonized by the shelter's trainer and much of the staff, who took his lead. She was deemed a difficult dog — blacklisted.

Undoubtedly, she had developed a guarded exterior. Considering her past, it was a necessary survival mechanism. Abandoned by her owners. Seized by the police as a stray. Twice scheduled to be euthanized at a municipal pound. Adopted and returned. And finally rescued by Great Tails, where she lived for nearly two years. It's no surprise that she became increasingly distrustful of people. She was also becoming more despondent with each passing day. In fact, she had deteriorated to the point that she rarely made eye contact. It was not unusual to hear shelter workers say, "She needs to get out of here." But there was no hope for that since she had been labeled by the shelter's trainer as an untrainable, unpredictable, aggressive dog, with a "screw loose." But with me she was a gentle, trusting, albeit occasionally headstrong, happy soul.

The sudden barking of the dogs in their kennels interrupted our love-fest and announced that the elderly man was returning after a 20-minute absence. Except for carrying his head a bit lower, he appeared exactly the same as we had seen earlier — with one difference — his flowers were gone.

The grounds behind the wooded area into which he had disappeared were dotted with small tombstones. The cemetery was called "The Memorial." It was reserved for dogs who had lived at the shelter. Some were fortunate to have been adopted. Others never made it out the front gates. All had found their final resting place at The Memorial.

As if scripted, the elderly gentleman and I simultaneously looked toward each other. Our eyes met and I nodded my head, letting him know I understood, or so I thought. Perhaps I was simply in denial, but in that moment, despite having previously experienced it, I was certain that the inevitable loss of a pet and subsequent grieving was something that only happened to others. Or perhaps I needed to disconnect from that eventuality so that I could move forward with my adoption of Pepper.

On a summer's eve nearly a decade later, the recollection of a frail, old man paying homage to his beloved dog with flowers left at a gravesite scattered through my mind as I was lying in the grass with my arm around a sleeping Pepper. In 20 minutes — after 8 1/2 wonderful, loving, sometimes challenging but always eventful years together — our journey was about to come to an end. A veterinarian was coming to my home to euthanize Pepper. And part of me.

Buddi

Siberian Huskies — majestic, masked Zorro look-alike dogs, projecting as much mystery as Johnston McCulley's original fictional character. Smitten the first time I saw one, I was somewhat obsessed with the idea of having one in my life. But as an adult, my absolute disinterest in the huge responsibility and obligation that accompanies dog ownership rendered my fantasy of owning a Siberian Husky an impossibility that was best served by remaining a fantasy.

I *did* have a tropical fish, a Betta named Jeffrey who, because those small Betta fish bowls looked like cruel round prisons, lived alone in 20-gallon tank. Jeffrey was the low-maintenance Yin to the Yang of my limited parenting skills. But truth be told, he wasn't very good at fetching, and I knew that taking him for a walk would likely not provide a happy ending. In short, he was as bad a substitute for a Siberian Husky as "New" Coke was for Classic Coke in the mid-'80s.

One morning while reading the Sunday news, I stumbled across a Parkdale Animal Shelter adoption ad. The PAS, situated on the south shore of Long Island, shelters dogs and cats. Right there, smack in the middle of the page was a picture of a black and white face-masked kitten. "Interesting," I thought, "a Siberian Husky kitten." Even though parenting a cat was not on my things-to-do list, I did feel as if I had passed the prerequisite course, Tropical Fish Parenting 101. Before you could say "Jeffrey ain't gonna be happy about this," I was out the door, on my way to adopting a feline Siberian Husky.

When I arrived at the shelter, I was struck by the size of the facility. It was no less than gigantic — a sad statement about how some people view their animals as disposable. Out of fear that someone was going to adopt my kitten before me, I hurried to the building that housed the cats and very quickly found my faux Siberian Husky. I excitedly summoned one of the adoption counselors and pointed, saying, "I'd like to adopt that one." With that, I dashed off to a room where prospective adopters meet their adoptee. Vibrating with anticipation, I waited to meet my new kid. The door opened and the counselor walked in with...the wrong kitten. Instead of my handsome, regal Husky cat, she placed a mangy, grey mess of a thing on the floor next to me. I was about to note the mistake, but couldn't. This shabby wreck of a kitten was never going to be adopted. I pictured her happily saying her farewells to all the other kittens on the way to the meeting room and how awful it would be to send her back. And so began the next 17 years of my life with Buddi, spelled as such because the counselor informed me that this scrawny grey kitten, if not exactly the cat I came for, was at least male, which I preferred. When Buddi and I visited the vet, I was otherwise enlightened — hence the more feminine spelling of "his" name.

Over the next several months, while transforming into a pretty cat, Buddi helped me gain an immense appreciation for tank-bound Jeffrey. It didn't take long for me to realize that the proverbial cheese had fallen off Buddi's cracker. She very much enjoyed climbing the curtains, chasing after me with claws out while swatting at my ankles, biting me to end petting sessions, and knocking over every item that wasn't nailed down. She routinely terrorized Jeffrey and houseguests, generally behaving like a certified mental case. Tropical Fish Parenting 101 was kindergarten compared to this.

Buddi at four years of age. She grew into a pretty cat.

At the low point of our "relationship," I placed an adoption ad in the same newspaper where I had seen my Siberian Husky cat. A day later, when a potential adopter called to inquire about her, much to my surprise I became very protective and said that she had already been taken. But the ad did serve a purpose. I cut it out of the newspaper and taped it to Buddi's food bowl, where it remained for the next 17 years: REMINDER: Behave yourself, or with one call you're outta here.

Of course, that call never happened, and it wasn't because Buddi suddenly became a model citizen. Instead, we learned to coexist and, in fact, I truly began to enjoy her different-ness, which included joining me in the shower every morning, playing fetch (yes, you can teach a cat to fetch), and playing hide-and-seek. I will admit she was a better hider than seeker. I'm pretty sure that at times, if I hadn't tipped her off to my clandestine location, I would have missed a few major holidays.

Toward the end of her life, along with other ailments, she went deaf and began losing her vision. Over the course of that year, I discovered, emotionally draining as it was, that caring for an elderly animal could be a profound and spiritually enhancing experience. And seemingly, Buddi discovered there was comfort to be found in being cared for. A beautiful, poetic symmetry framed our relationship.

On a snowy Christmas Eve, after watching her struggle to navigate the house, tripping over things, and looking terribly frightened and stressed, I was no longer able to rationalize that keeping her alive was humane. I brought Buddi to an emergency clinic to have her put down. Merry Christmas.

My 17 years with Buddi left me with a few powerful impressions. 1: Even though we refer to dogs and cats as "domesticated," they're animals first, deserving of respect for their animal-ness, and given the latitude to be themselves. When I embraced this, Buddi and I got along much better and built a powerful bond. 2: In hindsight, I suspected that the shelter's counselor had me pegged for a sucker and intentionally brought me the "wrong" cat, knowing I'd not have the heart to reject her. To this day, it's a great source of pride that she saw me in that light. 3: I would never bring another animal into my home. While Buddi wasn't a burden, the weight of responsible pet ownership, and the impact it has on one's life, was not going to get a second act in mine. Worse still, the unspeakable pain caused by the euthanasia of my feline child was something to which I vowed I would never again subject myself.

Unbeknownst to me at the time, my 17 years with a slightly unhinged Buddi — a cat with little chance of being adopted, whom I learned to understand, respect, and love — and my end-of-life caregiving for her, were a dress rehearsal for a future life with a very damaged, misunderstood, and unwanted shelter dog.

Jan and the 20 Paws of Mayhem

In 2002, single people were every bit as driven to meet their perfect match as were cavemen who tried to impress future brides by rubbing two sticks together to start a fire. Fortunately, I wasn't alive in the era of Neanderthals, as my relationship with fire has always been a curious one. I discovered this after the purchase of my first home, with my decision in part being driven by the existence of a fireplace in the den. From what I knew growing up, only rich people had fireplaces in their homes. I might not have been a rich person, but I could now enjoy one of their spoils — a roaring fireplace. Unfortunately, over time I learned that in my case, whatever talent was required to light a fire was missing from my life-skills box. Despite my disappointment, after several unsuccessful attempts to ignite a flame that lasted longer than a horny male rabbit, I gave up. I was also concerned that my attempts to ignite the logs would result in my home being burned down, with the fireplace the only thing left standing — populated with pristine, unlit logs. When I was ready to take the dating plunge, I chose the non-flammable, stay-at-home option, an online dating site called "YouDate."

"What fun," I thought. "I can go shopping for a mate without leaving my living room, or setting myself ablaze." I cranked up my speedy AOL connection and waited. After what felt like about 11 hours, I engaged the site's search tool, entered my criteria and clicked the search button. Up popped a picture of a beautiful blonde woman. Even though she lived in Connecticut, several miles from my Long Island home, I was not deterred. I thought of something charming and clever to say like, "Oh, so I see you live in Connecticut," entered the words into the "message" field, and clicked the *send* button.

Immediately after, a notification appeared informing me that before interacting with any site member, I first needed to make a payment. "Ah. I see how this works," said the skeptic in me. "As a lure, the site shows a picture of a gorgeous woman, and then requires payment to contact her." I surmised that, instead of being a member of the site, she was simply a photographic siren's song that the site used to entice us latter day, fire-phobic cavemen to fork over our money. But smitten as I was by Cupid's Connecticutian arrow, I made the payment. To my amazement, I received a response to my message. The ensuing online conversation lasted for several hours, until 3 AM. Jan was not only pretty; she was engaging, upbeat, and smart. We eventually met in person, hit it off, and began to date.

On a sunny Saturday afternoon in May, I made the first of several journeys north to Jan's home in Branford, Connecticut. With excited anticipation, I walked the curved path leading to the entrance of her home just as Jan, and five chaotic, charging dogs, exited the front door to "greet" me.

The 20 Paws of Mayhem. L-R, Cleo, Emily, BB, Jasmine, Hercules.

I don't recall if Jan had forewarned me about the 20 Paws of Mayhem Greeting I'd be receiving, but truth be told, it wouldn't have made much of a difference. There are things in life we simply can't prepare for, and one of them is five large dogs wildly circling you in a way that would make the Tasmanian Devil envious. Their simultaneous crazed barking was the icing on an extremely nerve-racking cake. From an evolutionary perspective, we aren't far enough removed from the days when animals considered us lunch for such a greeting to be met with quiet dignity and grace. Not wanting to look like a wimp, I employed the *silent scream* coping method, thanked my lucky stars that I didn't need to pee, and waited for either my life or the barking to end.

Having survived the initial greeting, over time I would learn that Jasmine, Hercules, Cleo, BB, and Emily were five wonderful dogs.

Jasmine struck me as the Aretha Franklin, Queen of Soul of the group. She was elegant and sophisticated while being a delightfully playful German Shepherd. Etched in my memory is a frigid winter morning when I was pitching shovels of snow over my shoulder, unaware that "Jaz" was standing a few feet behind me, reveling in the joy of being buried alive. Light-hearted, yet very grounded, she was the group's moral compass.

Hercules was also a German Shepherd and cousin of Jasmine. Living with five females, the poor guy never stood a chance. It didn't help that his name was a lot to live up to. One afternoon while Jan was out running errands, I taught "Herc" to come to what I deemed a more fitting name, one that sounded less heroic and was a better fit for his personality, "Truman." Jan wasn't impressed. Daily, he accepted his fate in a good-natured, delightfully dopey manner. But for all his goofy behaviors, he was one handsome, graceful dog. He was the dog most likely to be elected the group's mascot.

Cleo, a Weimaraner who Jan insisted was grey, rather than the brown dog that I saw, was a loving ball of energy. When happy, she didn't wag her tail, she wagged her *entire* body, vibrating like a tuning fork. She had a serious snuggling addiction and was a definite Momma's dog. Cleo and I quietly vied for Jan's attention. Rightly so, I usually came up with the short end of the bone. Cleo's unbridled passion for life was without parallel. She was the eternal puppy of the group.

BB, Big and Beautiful, was a dog's dog. While the others in the group seemingly possessed a few human qualities, BB would have none of that. Watching her launch her 90-pound, shiny black-coated body into the air to intercept a Frisbee was a sight to behold. Of the five, she was by far the most ambivalent about me. "I really like him. But maybe not. It's nice when he's here. But I hope he's leaving soon. I think I'll go over to him. On second thought, this couch is very comfortable." BB was the true dog of the group.

Emily was BB's delicate and dainty sister. Unfortunately, I didn't get to know her well. When she reached adolescence, fights began to break out between the female dogs. Sadly, this is not an unusual occurrence, as the most risk-filled pairing, other than intact males, is two female dogs. In these situations, sometimes rehoming is the best, and only, option. The happy ending to Emily's story was that, through Canine Companions, she was adopted by a family with a developmentally challenged boy. She lived out her life in the lap of luxury on Manhattan's Upper West Side, with multiple daily trips to the scenic waterfront of Riverside Park.

My interaction with the 20 Paws of Mayhem was a road-to-Damascus revelation, teaching me that dogs aren't black-box-driven machines. They all possess unique personalities, and while sharing many common traits, thrive when treated as individuals. And as individuals, our interactions with them are most rewarding and meaningful when we don't see them as subservient to us. Recalling the lessons I learned from Buddi, Jan's dogs reminded me that even "domesticated" animals are, first and foremost, animals, and they flourish when we allow them the room to be their natural selves.

My time spent with the 20 Paws of Mayhem shaped my perspectives as a trainer and how I would later parent Pepper.

Mira

Kurt Vonnegut once said, "Enjoy the little things in life because one day you'll look back and realize they were the big things." To this day I am unsure of what motivated me, but one such *little thing* occurred during one of my stays in Branford — I asked Jan if I could take Jasmine for a walk. I had never walked a dog before. Engulfed in a swirl of excitement and nervousness, I attached a leash to her collar and embarked on a journey that would forever change me. Despite being a large German Shepherd tipping the scales at over 90 pounds, as we made our way through the pastoral countryside, I felt as if there was nothing at the end of the leash but cotton candy. We were harmoniously synchronized, in perfect step, without a word being spoken. Even as I write this so many years later, the magic of that walk is still with me. I feel immense gratitude toward Jasmine, for my walk with her jump-started my drive to become a dog trainer, and more significantly, indirectly led to my adoption of Pepper.

I was hooked. Within a very short time, my bookshelves were jam-packed with dog training manuals, books, and guides. My television, which formerly only shared a weekly relationship with the Dallas Cowboys, through DVD lectures found new friends named Dunbar, McConnell, Sdao, Wilde, and Ali Brown — major figures in the field of positive-reinforcement dog training. No doubt the books and DVDs were helpful, but one can only learn so much through a monologue. I doubt that anyone has learned how to play the piano solely by reading a book called "How to Play the Piano." I needed a mentor and some hands-on experience.

On June 21, 2008, a few months after my lighter-than-air dance with Jasmine, I sent an email to a local trainer, Mira Leibstein, inquiring if she'd be willing to mentor me. In other words, I was asking her to teach a stranger to possibly become her competition, not exactly a great sales pitch on my part.

Hi Mira.

I am a member of the APDT aspiring to a new career as a dog trainer. I am in the process of self-teaching and have recently applied to Great Tails Animal Shelter for volunteer work.

I have read 15 or so training books and also have a dozen or so books on CD, which I listen to in my car.

I was wondering if there would be a chance you'd be willing to speak with me about mentoring me.

Thank you VERY much for your time.

John

Much to my delight, and equally to my surprise, Mira responded. A few days later, we met at a local Starbucks, where we conversed and instantly connected. She was funny, light-hearted, brilliant, and very knowledgeable about the field of training. After our initial meeting, I received the following email:

John,

It was wonderful to spend some time with someone "on the same wavelength" so to speak. You know how unusual that can be…keep in touch! It gets lonely working on your own as a trainer, and it's great to bounce thoughts off friends and share those lightbulb moments with people who understand!

Elation is the only word that could describe my reaction. Mira saw me as being "on the same wavelength." It was like Neil Armstrong telling a kid on a tricycle that they were on the same wavelength.

Not only did she agree to mentor me, Mira extended an invitation to assist her when she provided training services at a shelter in Great Neck, Long Island. Aware that she was putting her reputation on the line by doing so, I wanted to assure her that I wasn't a dunce (looking back I was, in fact, a dunce with a capital DUNCE). I offered to answer any training questions she posed.

In response she asked, "Which end of the dog is the leash attached to?" and "Which end of the dog has teeth?" I replied by inquiring if the test was open-book and if she'd be grading with a curve. The questions were Mira's way of saying that she had full faith in me — which felt great. She was also providing a valuable lesson — when training, don't become arrogant and don't complicate things.

As with so many scripted coincidences that aligned perfectly with my journey into dog training, and crossing paths with Pepper, my relationship with Mira was a godsend. For the better part of a year, I shadowed her on appointments and assisted during group classes, gaining invaluable experience about positive-reinforcement training from the ground up. I have her to thank for teaching me much of what I know about the field of training, including which end of the dog has teeth.

Who Knows What Is Good and What is Bad

As noted in my initial email to Mira, in June of 2008 I applied for volunteer work at Great Tails, in large part due to its excellent reputation. In much the same manner as I had contacted Mira, I provided the Great Tails trainer a laundry list of the books, DVDs, and audiobooks in my collection. I also mentioned that I was hoping to shadow and be mentored by a CPDT (Certified Professional Dog Trainer), Mira. Surprisingly, I didn't receive a response to my email. I emailed a second time, and again, did not receive a response. I called and left a message, to no avail. And with that, I gave up.

Several weeks passed and, with a renewed sense of purpose, I again chose to try my hand at volunteer work. Because I had not received a response from Great Tails, even though it was much farther from my home I decided to apply for volunteer work at the Parkdale Animal Shelter — the shelter from which I adopted Buddi. Based on my nonstarter experience with Great Tails, I figured an in-person application would provide a better outcome. After doing some research about the facility, a few days later, I headed over, only to be confronted with a traffic jam that was epic even by Long Island standards. As I inched toward the last exit that offered an escape route back to my home, I made a life-altering decision. Instead of going home, I chose to drive north to Great Tails.

Having been employed as a salesperson for years, I knew the value of persistence — keep trying or starve. With that mindset, I was resolved to not leave Great Tails until I had been hired as a volunteer. Visible from the parking lot, off to the side of the kennels in Building One, a bright green sign announced the location of the main office. Little did I know that the last kennel on the right housed a dog who would forever change my life. Once inside the office, I was warmly greeted by a woman sitting at a desk. I explained my situation and mentioned the numerous attempts I had made to contact the shelter's trainer. Her surprise and displeasure were clearly evident. "The shelter is *always* looking for volunteers," she said as she reached for an application. "And given your knowledge, you'd be a great addition."

I completed the application and was invited to an orientation meeting later that week. Mission accomplished — I was officially a volunteer at Great Tails. In hindsight, I am reminded of Taoist parable entitled "Who Knows What Is Good and What Is Bad."

When an old farmer's stallion wins a prize at a country show, his neighbor calls round to congratulate him, but the old farmer says, "Who knows what is good and what is bad?"

The next day some thieves come and steal his valuable animal. His neighbor comes to commiserate with him, but the old man replies, "Who knows what is good and what is bad?"

A few days later the spirited stallion escapes from the thieves and joins a herd of wild mares, leading them back to the farm. The neighbor calls to share the farmer's joy, but the farmer says, "Who knows what is good and what is bad?"

The following day, while trying to break in one of the mares, the farmer's son is thrown and fractures his leg. The neighbor calls to share the farmer's sorrow, but the old man's attitude remains the same as before.

The following week the army passes by, forcibly conscripting soldiers for the war, but they do not take the farmer's son because he cannot walk. The neighbor thinks to himself, "Who knows what is good and what is bad?" and realizes that the old farmer must be a Taoist sage.

If not for a traffic jam, and the rejections at Great Tails —which made me even more determined to volunteer there — I'd never have met Pepper.

Who knows what is good and what is bad.

"OK, Pepper. Please Give Me a Sit"

It wasn't a heavy snowfall, but enough that I suspected rather than brave the elements, many shelter volunteers would stay home for the day. It seemed the perfect opportunity for my dog walking debut. If things went awry, there'd be no witnesses.

Imagine my delight when I arrived at the snow-covered grounds and found a Siberian Husky named Zyna in need of a walk. Facilities like Great Tails don't typically house pure-bred dogs. And given my decades-old love for Siberian Huskies, the fact that I'd be walking one on my maiden voyage clearly made me feel as if predestination was in the air. I later discovered it was — but in that moment, I had tuned in to the wrong channel.

The walk went well. In fact, unbeknownst to me, we were being observed by a shelter veteran named Mike who, as we returned from our walk, approached and offered, "You guys were a thing of beauty. Ya know, you're both new here. Yesterday was her first day here."

I elected to quit while I was ahead, and didn't walk any other dogs that day. During the drive home, I thought about Zyna, in much the same manner as Jasmine after our maiden walk. To share my experience, I called my sister, who commented, "Are you going to adopt her?" to which I replied, "Not a chance. It's way too much of a responsibility. I'm at the shelter to learn about dogs, not adopt one."

When I returned to the shelter two days later, after signing in at the front office, flush with anticipation I went directly to Zyna's kennel to say hello. It was empty. Someone had adopted her. So much for predestination — or so I thought.

Back at the office, I checked the scheduling board to see which dogs needed a walk. Those who had been walked recently were identified by the time of the walk, written next to their names on a dry-erase scheduling board. Blank spaces indicated which dogs were next. Spotting the first vacancy, I made note of the kennel number and dog's name, grabbed a leash, and headed on over. Housed in the kennel at the end of the Building One (the same building where I had applied for volunteer work) was a dog who greeted me in true Looney Tunes fashion. She was jumping straight up in the air, much like cartoon characters do prior to taking off in a mad dash. With a smile on my face that mirrored the one in my heart, I made a request: "OK, Pepper. Please give me a sit."

Just like Zyna, Pepper did not resemble a typical shelter dog. Yes, she was a mutt (I use the term with great affection) but an elegant one, with many physical characteristics of an Australian Shepherd. Even in her cage, she projected a regal air about her and yet at the same time, she looked adorably sweet. Her coat was long and unruly in a few spots, mostly black, highlighted by bronze and auburn, along with a snow-white patch on her chest. Her tail was plush, like a large beautiful feather duster. Her ears folded forward, with the left one flopping a bit to the side. But her most striking feature was her eyes. All who met her were captivated by her rich chestnut-colored eyes. The fur around them was a brownish tan, giving her the appearance of wearing goggles. But there was more to them than a picture or description could ever convey. If eyes are the gateway to the soul, her gates were wide open. During her time at the shelter they were tinged with a deep melancholy, which reflected her emotional state. I would later learn that when she disapproved of something or found a request to be frivolous, her expressive eyes would communicate a somewhat bemused and gentle tolerance. "You're kidding me, right?" seemed to emanate from them. Those who got to know her were familiar with what we referred to as *The Look.* It was a peculiar honor to be a recipient of *The Look.*

The Look.

After a few repetitions of *dog on an invisible pogo stick,* Pepper heeded my request and sat. I opened the kennel gate, attached the leash to her collar, and off we went. I wish I could remember more about that first walk. I'm assuming it was fairly uneventful, which, from what I would later learn about Pepper, was an event in and of itself.

With our walk completed, I returned to the office. As I was hanging the leash on a rack I commented to one of the staff, "Ya know what Wile E. Coyote looks like when the stick of dynamite explodes? I just walked a dog who looks a bit like that." She replied, "Oh, that's Pepper. The groomer was here yesterday." Teasingly, I commented, "Tell her to use more mousse next time."

Later that night as I was lying in bed, I pictured Pepper in her darkened kennel. I thought of what it must have been like to be her, locked in a cage for 20-plus hours each day for hundreds of days.

I did a lot more thinking than sleeping that night.

Ulster Avenue, Mexican Food, and Recovery

No one knew much about the first three years of Pepper's life. She had been abandoned by her owners 15 miles from her home in Uniondale, Long Island. She roamed the streets until September 14, 2007, when she was seized by a police officer at the corner of Ulster Avenue in Babylon. The only ID she carried was a rabies tag that hung from a tattered collar. Through the ID number on the tag, the municipal pound identified her owners. Repeated attempts to contact them went unanswered. The final communication informed her owners she would be euthanized if not claimed — still no response. Fortunately, she was adopted by an elderly gentleman, but sadly, was returned a few days later due to "behavioral issues." She had also been diagnosed as heartworm positive by her adopter's veterinarian. Upon reentry into the municipal pound, she was again placed on the euthanasia list. She escaped that fate when, on November 9, 2007, she was rescued by Great Tails.

She arrived at Great Tails weighing just 26 pounds, approximately half of her healthy weight. Fatigue and labored breathing would set in even after the shortest of walks — clearly the heartworms were taking their toll. Her disease was graded Class III, the most severe. She was already demonstrating advanced symptoms, and if not treated immediately, her life would soon come to an end.

Left: A 26-pound Pepper during her early days at Great Tails. Right: In my back yard six months after I adopted her.

Inappetence is often present in the advanced stages of the disease, and Pepper wasn't an exception — she displayed little interest in eating. Purely by chance, the few who were dedicated to her discovered she loved Mexican food. Every day at mealtime, one of the staff would make a Mexican food run. Despite a horrible first few years of life, she did have her blessings. Those who cared for her at the shelter, especially during those early days, could be counted among them.

To restrict her activity while being treated, Pepper was housed in the shelter's office rather than a kennel. Too much activity can lead to heartworms splitting off into other areas of the body. Even after heartworms die, an overly active dog can cause them to travel into the arteries and cause blockages. It was imperative to monitor her and limit her activity.

Within a few months, Pepper was in good physical health. Her veterinarian's report notes this, as well as a gain in weight and a side comment, "Pepper needs to be muzzled during all exams." A few months later, an entry in another report states, "Dog would not allow examination of hindquarters even while wearing muzzle." Given her history, it's not surprising that Pepper had trust issues. One of her caregivers, Anne, summed her up perfectly:

I was thinking about it all day yesterday and I came up with a thought about Pepper which is why she was so unique. Dogs, we are told, give unconditional love and welcome it in return. That is true enough, but Pepper wanted more. She wanted RESPECT, and only respected those who gave it to her. Maybe her first years made her realize if she didn't stand up for herself and demand respect, she was not going to get it. I admire her so much for that. You respected her from day one and let her be Pepper, with quirks and all. And so, she respected you, with all your quirks. That respect grew into such a love and such a bond. Like all good relationships, it was based on respect and trust.

And this from another of Pepper's favorite caregivers, Louise:

She was as sweet to me as anything and unlike others, I never had a fear of her. I always referred to her as a graceful brat. She did get kind of spunky with other dogs, and stupid people, but she just needed someone to be her director. And that turned out to be you.

By November of 2007, over a year before I met her, Pepper had been nursed back to physical health.

Her emotional well-being was entirely another story.

"There's a Dog Inside That Dog"

In the days following our first walk together, Pepper and I quickly began to build a bond. On weekdays, dressed in a suit and tie on my way home from work, I'd visit the shelter to walk and spend time with her. Weekends became our favorite as our time wasn't restricted. Proverbial hell or high water, I wasn't going to be deterred from visiting her every day. Even while healing two broken toes on my right foot, I continued to visit and take her for walks just as I had before. She quickly became a priority in my life and a great "fix" for a sense of emptiness that had partnered with me since my childhood.

My routine upon arriving at the shelter was to sign in and then immediately check the scheduling board. If Pepper had already been walked, when no one was looking, like a misbehaving child I'd erase the entry next to her name, and with leash in hand, happily make my way over to her kennel. Knowing she'd thrive with some training, I snuck contraband Nabisco animal crackers into the shelter. Volunteers were permitted to feed only carrots to the dogs, which Pepper liked about as much as I did — not at all. There's a saying in the field of training: "No motivation. No training." The pursuit of animal crackers provided Pepper with motivation, and they just happened to be a favorite of mine. I also brought a device known as a *clicker,* a training tool frowned upon by the shelter's trainer. The clicker, a small plastic gadget that emits a "click" sound when triggered, is a positive-reinforcement training tool rooted in B.F. Skinner's work in the 1950s. The "click" is used to "mark" the desired behavior, after which a reinforcement is presented to strengthen the behavior. Thanks to Mira's tutelage, I had become quite proficient with the device.

My initial training goal was to help Pepper regain enough confidence to make direct eye contact with me. While living mostly in isolation at the shelter, her willingness to make eye contact diminished almost to the point of being nonexistent. Sitting side by side on one of the shelter benches, removed from the main flow of traffic, I simply waited without speaking or interacting with her. Whenever she made any motion in my direction, I would mark the behavior with a click and, while not turning toward her lest I make her nervous, reinforce the behavior with an animal cracker. Doing so helped Pepper to realize, "Every time I look at him, it somehow makes the clicker go off and I get a treat. This isn't so spooky after all. In fact, it's fun."

A few days after we began our eye contact exercises, during one of our sessions Pepper turned toward me and licked the side of my face. While this was clearly a sign of progress, I didn't realize just how big a step it was for her. In fact, it was the *only* time, including the 8 ½ years that we lived together, that she licked me without my luring the behavior. Yes, I will admit to occasionally cheapening myself, when out of desperation I would shamelessly spread peanut butter on my face to entice her.

After Pepper became comfortable making voluntary eye contact, we proceeded to the next step in our training, the development of a "watch" cue, where she'd learn to provide eye contact upon request. Within a few short minutes, the dog who had avoided all eye contact for months perfected her "watch" cue. In heartening fashion, during our years together, she would often sit and stare at me. "Whatever happened to the dog who wouldn't even look at me?" I'd say in faux-exasperation. "Would you please stop staring at me?!"

With our first goal met, we then focused on basic trick training, a fun activity that, by providing life enrichment, would be great for her self-confidence and offer mental stimulation. Because training is most effective with minimal distractions, I earned clearance to take her to an area called "the field," away from the chaos of the shelter buildings. The field was a double-fenced acre where, in the company of a volunteer who had gone through a short training period, dogs were allowed off leash, one at a time. While there, we worked on basic cues and fun tricks like jumping over a hand-held branch. Pepper was a quick learner. When performing, the traces of melancholy in her eyes vanished, replaced by a confetti display of sparkling brightness. One morning on our way back from the field, I couldn't resist showing off her branch-jumping skills to a group of volunteers and shelter employees, including the shelter's trainer. Much to their delight, Pepper performed her "sit/stay/jump" cue flawlessly. The only person who wasn't impressed was the shelter's trainer, who frowned and walked away while others were applauding. In that moment, with Pepper's transition from the dog he had demonized and given up on to this burgeoning version of who she truly was, he should have celebrated like the others. He didn't. His loss.

Pepper's transformation surprised a lot of people, but not me. From the first day I met her, despite her reputation I thought, "There's a dog inside that dog."

Yellow Dot

Similar to other shelters, based on the behavioral makeup of each dog, Great Tails utilized a color-coded classification system. Green-dot dogs were permitted to be walked by anyone. Yellow-dot dogs could only be walked by certified volunteers. And red-dot dogs were off limits to all but certified shelter employees. Two days after Pepper's branch-jumping demonstration, I arrived at the shelter and learned that her status had changed from green to yellow dot. According to shelter rules, I was no longer allowed to walk or interact with her. Additionally, the change in her status further lessened the already very slim chances of her being adopted. Color coding was shown on each dog's kennel card, visible to potential adopters. With so many dogs available, it wasn't likely that an adopter would choose a yellow-dot "problem" dog over a more easily managed one. When I inquired about Pepper's reclassification, I was informed that the trainer claimed she was becoming aggressive with men and others she could "take advantage of" (whatever that means) while on leash.

Without voicing any irritation, or suspicions about the reclassification, I dutifully inquired as to how volunteers became yellow-dot certified. I was informed that the shelter's trainer held certification classes. Determined not to allow Pepper to regress, I enrolled in the class, and even though I was not yet certified to do so, I continued to walk her anyway. Pepper and I held some similar views about authority figures. A few weeks later, I attended the class, and gained my yellow-dot certification.

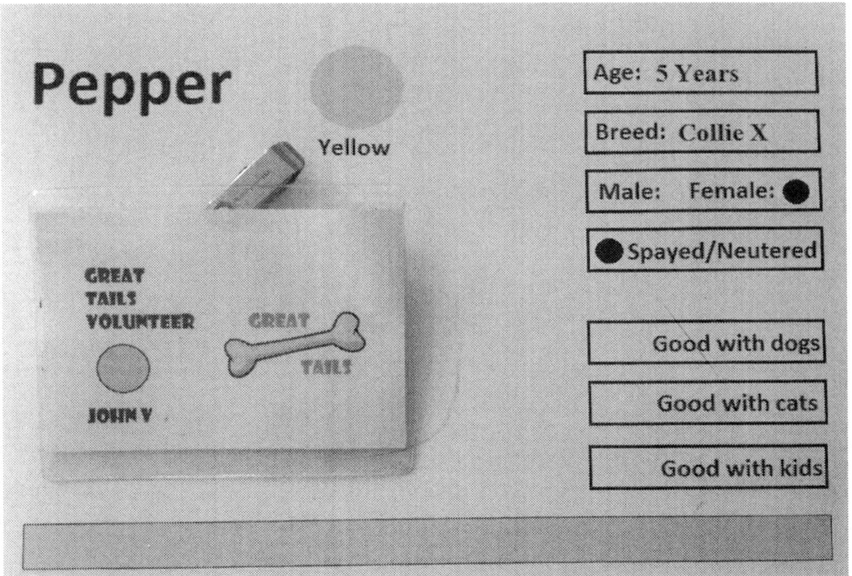

My yellow-dot badge and Pepper's kennel ID card. Note how the card classifies her.

The following day, newly yellow-dot certified, I arrived at the shelter for my daily Pepper session. One of her favorite people, a long-time shelter employee named Matt, had just placed her food bowl in front of her. He greeted me and lamented, "Sorry. She just started to eat. She'll come out to you when she's done." On a hunch I said, "I think she'll come to me anyway." A smiling Matt, who dearly loved Pepper and knew her well, replied, "If she does, it'll be the first time I've ever seen a shelter dog do that." And with that, much to Matt's delight, Pepper, who always greeted me like toast popping out of a toaster, saw me and came running over, leaving her food behind as we exited her kennel.

Clearly, something extraordinary was happening between this remarkably different dog and me.

Finding Home

In early 2009, the so-called Great Recession was in full bloom. Median household incomes had dropped 35% since the beginning of the decline over a year earlier. Unemployment rose to 10%, with almost 9 million jobs lost in that time frame. Home values plummeted, the stock market lost over 50% of its value — and there was no end in sight.

At the time, I was employed as a salesperson in the commercial printing industry. As a money-saving measure, my customers began using the internet rather than printed materials to promote their businesses. I would have been fortunate to only lose 35% of my income. Instead, in just 15 months, my income dropped over 70%.

Through it all, Pepper was a life-saver, providing value beyond any amount of money, and despite my previous ironclad conviction to never adopt another animal, I was inching down the emotional path to doing so. But there was much to consider. Pepper was not the kind of dog who would do well in an apartment, and given my declining financial health, I was concerned that I would need to sell my home. But, I reminded myself, apartment life would be a vast upgrade from living in a cage. I was also worried that I'd be working 50 hours a week and that, if I adopted her, she'd be alone for very long periods of time. Again, I reminded myself that being alone for 50 hours in my home would be a notable improvement for her. Finally, regardless of any limitations and complications, I knew she wasn't going to end up in a better home than I could provide. After 21 months at the shelter, it was painfully clear she had been sentenced to living there for the rest of her life.

During one of my shelter visits, I overheard a staffer comment about someone who surrendered their dog because they were moving, "I'd live in my car with my dog before doing that." I couldn't envision being so dedicated and yet, the comment resonated like a vibrating tuning fork in a part of my soul that had been lying dormant. Logic said that this was not the time to bring a dog into my life. But logic was never the GPS for my journey with Pepper.

Whenever I was confronted with a difficult situation, my dad, who was not a man of many words, would comment in a reassuring tone, "You'll figure it out." The way he spoke those few words framed my mindset when I sent an email to Mira on March 28, 2009:

So…uh…I think I fell in love.

This dog, Pepper (pictures attached), from Great Tails, is brilliant and has bonded with me in a very unique way. She's a tough handle for some of the others there, but with me she's perfect…I think I might bring her home…Oh my.

Mira responded:

Oh, you're done for. She's fabulous, crazy gene and all. Is this the one with whom you had issues with other volunteers? Congrats, welcome to parenthood…

For reasons not fully apparent at the time, Pepper and I had already developed a strong bond. I later came to realize that I felt a connection to her because I could relate to her due to my own history. There's nothing deadlier than someone droning on about their life story, so I'll spare you the in-depth details about my youth in the hopes that someday, if you write a book, you will return the favor. But I *will* chronicle those years just enough to illustrate the similarities between Pepper and me.

As a youngster, I was always uncomfortable interacting with others, mostly because I rarely found common ground on which to do so. Often, that discomfort was misinterpreted, leading people to see me in a negative light. As a result, much like Pepper, to shield myself I was very selective about whom I allowed close to me. Over time, this became an almost reflexive behavior, resulting in even greater isolation. I joke about it today but as evidence of this, my high school yearbook wasn't signed by anyone. To this day, I have no idea why I even *bought* a yearbook. A yearbook in my hands made about as much sense as giving a bicycle to a turtle. As further evidence, I spent school lunch periods wandering the halls rather than suffering the embarrassment of sitting by myself, or worse yet, being rejected when attempting to join others. Many years later, still somewhat isolated, during my walks with Pepper I'd recall the emotions of that kid wandering the halls, only now I was accompanied by my best friend, someone who provided me with a sense of belonging. I hoped I was doing the same for her.

Pepper's untapped potential was something to which I could easily relate. After scoring very well on several aptitude tests as a child, I was enrolled in advanced learning classes. And like Pepper, a very smart dog, without direction and support that potential was squandered. I concluded my high school years by graduating in the lower half of my class. I then dabbled in college for a short time and finally bailed on my education altogether. The way I figured, an education was probably important, but not if I had to go to school to get one. And so ended my years as a student.

And most painfully, like Pepper, whose owners had abandoned her, I didn't feel accepted in my own home. In fact, if I had the proverbial nickel for every time I heard my mother say, "We just didn't know what to do with you," I'd own a ton of proverbial nickels. A therapist friend once noted, "On the way to delivering you, the stork hiccupped over the wrong house."

Many years later, while strolling the grounds of an outdoor craft show, I purchased a black and gold Native American wish jar. Upon arriving home, I wrote a note, lifted the jar's lid and placed it inside. The note read *find home.* Over 20 years later, with that note still in the jar, *home found me* in the form of a misunderstood and previously unwanted, buried treasure of a shelter dog.

Essence

I wasn't entering Pepper parenthood blinded by love or with the expectation of a fairy tale journey. During one shelter visit, when I entered her kennel and knelt to pet her, surprisingly, she stiffened — never a good sign. A second later, she bit me. When she did, I noticed her body was over a pig's ear. She was guarding it. The vast majority of dogs who exhibit resource guarding do so out of insecurity — they fear someone is going to take their prized possession. Given her barren existence, a pig's ear was all the more valuable. In that moment with her insecurity having manifested itself, I felt badly for her. Because I also felt badly for me, I backed off and dejectedly said, "Ah c'mon, Pepps. I rushed here from work to be with you and that's what you do?"

Amazingly, she did something that, in all my years of training, I have never experienced with a resource guarding dog — she left the pig's ear and approached me. I petted her and let her know that I understood why she felt the need to do what she did. I also let her know that I appreciated that she had wonderful bite inhibition — she had bitten but didn't so much as leave a mark on my hand. Her bite was simply her way of communicating her distress — she didn't want to hurt me.

The model for how we would build a new life was set. I always respected the reasons for her behaviors — they had helped her to survive some very difficult years. But if we were going to be living together, she needed to learn more appropriate behaviors. Starting that day at the shelter, and continuing for months after she arrived in my home, we practiced multiple repetitions of behavior modification protocols — shelter dogs don't suddenly change because they feel indebted and appreciative for being rescued. Behavior modification is the result of respect for the dog as an emotional being, understanding canine behavior, viewing the dog as an animal instead of a pet, and consistent, repetitive training regimens.

Along with her proclivity for guarding items, another deeply concerning trait was the way Pepper would "zone out" when something caught her attention. In an email to Mira I noted, "I swear, I could fire a bazooka next to her when she's fixated on something, and it wouldn't faze her in the least." Behavior modification isn't possible without first capturing the dog's attention. This would be no mean feat with Pepper.

Ultimately, none of it mattered. I knew at her essence she was a damn good dog. With patience, practice, and building of trust, I could reach her. She had already reached me. The least I could do was return the favor.

Matt

To prepare for adopting her, and to allow my logical brain to catch up with the rest of me, I requested that Pepper be placed on "adoption hold." The hold allowed me right of first refusal should someone express interest in adopting her. Unlikely as that was, the more I got to know her, the more I worried my prize would be discovered. I was also permitted to take her home on weekends. Home visits helped break the monotony of her day-to-day life at the shelter and provided me with the opportunity to devise a solid transition plan.

As word of the adoption hold filtered out to the staff, many assumed I would not follow through. After all, Pepper was a "difficult" dog. But Pepper's friend Matt knew better. One day, upon seeing me enter the building that housed Pepper, he ran to greet me. The laws of physics would suggest that his feet were in contact with the ground, but his demeanor suggested otherwise.

Beaming with jubilance he exclaimed, "I heard you're thinking of adopting Pepper! She's the smartest dog here, always has been. She's a great dog!" As Matt spoke, his body language was very similar to Pepper's pogo-stick greetings. He was literally bouncing up and down. Matt and Pepper were truly kindred spirits who shared a unique, soulful relationship, as is evident in an email that Matt sent sometime after I adopted her:

The weird thing is, I can still feel the rush of happiness I felt when I first heard that you were going to adopt Pepper. It's not just a memory either, I actually feel it each and every time I think about it. I feel it now just writing about it.

Sometimes in life you get something you really, REALLY want and it's so much better than you EVER EVEN imagined. It doesn't happen very often but when it does, you never forget it and how spectacular it feels. This was one of those kind of happenings.

A while back you asked me to write down anything I remember about Pepper and her days at Great Tails because you wanted to know everything about her life before the two of you met. I told you I would do it, but I never did. It wasn't that I forgot or didn't have time to do it. The real reason I never did it is because there was far too much sadness and too many painful negative elements surrounding her stay there. They were dark days for her and I knew it. I knew that each day was a struggle for her just to exist. I knew that each day she became more and more unhappy and hopeless. I know this may sound crazy and strange, but every time I touched her I could feel the unbearable pain she was in — like it was transmitted from her body into mine. I used to try and pet the sadness out of her.

Then along came you.

I remember the first time I saw you show up and take her for a walk. You were all dressed up and I remember thinking how cool it was that you didn't much care about your nice clothes getting dirty, or getting dog hair on them, and that even though you had important stuff to do, this was just as important to you. I remember seeing you come back again and again, each time going straight for Pepper upon your arrival. I remember how sweetly you spoke to her when you greeted her and how you always spoke to her with such kindness. I remember how much time you spent with her and how many things you would do with her. I remember thinking how much time and energy you devoted to her, instead of the quick 10-minute walk most people gave. I remember how she forgot I was there when you walked in the room. I remember how happy I was that my friend Pepper had a true friend to help her want to live again. I remember how happy she would be when I would see the two of you in the distance. I remember how she would almost be dancing as she returned to the kennel with you. I remember how she absorbed and relished every second she got to spend with you. I remember how she looked after you would leave for the day, and I remember thinking that because of that time and love you gave her, she could make it through another day. I remember feeling so happy when you would walk into the place, because I knew you were going to make her the happiest dog in the kennels and that every second she got to spend with you would be the antidote to her heartbreaking struggle.

Then I heard "the news" about what you were planning. I ran around there like a kid who just got his first bike for Christmas, telling everyone who would listen the awesome news. I knew what was going to happen was more spectacular than my words could convey and I would just stand there, deliver the news to whomever would listen, and try to contain the happiness and excitement that was overwhelming me.

I reminded Pepper every day after that, that her wait was almost over. Some people thought you might not adopt her, but I KNEW and she KNEW that it was going to happen. And then it did! And Pepper's life truly started again.

The dark days are gone forever and she and you will always share what you had from day one together…a life-changing connection that healed so much sadness and desperation and replaced it with hope and love.

Those are the only memories that are important or that matter.

Those are my first memories of my friends Pepper and John.

25 Million Bucks Short of Yesterday

Shelter policy stated that prior to Pepper's first weekend visit, an examination of my home and yard was required. The inspection, conducted by the shelter's trainer, was scheduled for a Friday at 4 PM, and went off without a hitch. Immediately after, I dashed to my car and headed for the shelter. Oh boy!

Upon arriving at the shelter, I pulled into the parking lot on two wheels and slingshot myself out of the car. I hurried to the office and, upon entering, an administrator expressed surprise at seeing me. I was informed that the shelter's trainer would be bringing Pepper to my house for her first visit. A showdown was about to occur.

"That's not happening," I said, making no attempt to hide my displeasure. "I have only one chance to introduce her to my home, and no one other than me is going to do so." My comments were met with a raised eyebrow and a recitation of the shelter's policy. In response, I repeated *Visconti's* policy. Finally, after a few more exchanges, the shelter manager was summoned to the office. When she arrived, I again stated my objections and again heard about shelter policy. "OK. Have it your way. If I can't bring her home, you can remove the adoption hold," I bluffed as I turned toward the door and took a few steps, praying that someone would stop me. "Hold on." Sweeter words I had never heard. "Since this is a unique situation, and since you're a trainer, yes, you can take her home." A form was placed in front of me, requiring my signature. It could have stated that I agreed to have my nose twisted with a pair of pliers until it looked like a corkscrew. I signed without reading a single word and dashed out the door.

Pepper looked great in my red Corvette. She sat comfortably in the passenger seat as if we had done this dozens of times. During the ride, I treated her with her favorite animal crackers, and overjoyed, I sang my first original song about her.

Being a published songwriter who had survived the music biz, including all the inane and often insensitive critiques of my songs by publishers and producers, I found liberation while crooning to an accepting, nonjudgmental audience. In fact, I was permitted to invent words, force rhymes, and mangle melodies, without fear of recrimination.

Paul McCartney has often described the magic of channeling his song "Yesterday." He awoke one morning, went directly to his piano, and began playing a tune that came to him in a dream. There were no lyrics or title for the song. Since it was just before breakfast, as a reference, he dubbed it "Scrambled Eggs." Worried that he had subconsciously plagiarized his new creation, over the next few days McCartney hummed the melody for friends and relatives inquiring, "Is this a song? Have you heard it before?" When no one recognized the tune, he assumed he had written it. McCartney's channeled creation went on to earn him royalties of approximately $25 million. "Yesterday" holds the record for the song most covered by other performers — it has been recorded by more than 2,000 artists.

Not to compare myself to Paul, but on the way home that day, I sang a song to Pepper that I too channeled from the universe — a song that became a standard for us during the next 8 ½ years. And in all candor, it was a song that Pepper liked infinitely more than "Yesterday."

Pepper, Pepperino, you are super keen-o
Pepper, Pepperoni, you are my one and only
Pepper, Pepperelli, you are never smelly
Pepper, Peppernickle, my old heart you do tickle

Pepper, Pepper-eesta, you have a cute keister
Pepper, Peppasaurus, you don't use a thesaurus
Pepper, Pepperlicious, you are so delicious
Pepper Peppernickle, my old heart you doooOOOooOOOooOOoo tickle!

Not only did she love the lyrics (especially while I gave her animal crackers) but the melody seemed to meet with her approval as well. Undoubtedly, I had channeled a classic. The only thing missing was the 25 million bucks in royalties.

One other standard was fashioned during that initial drive home. While leaning with her left side against her seat, Pepper extended her left paw and wrapped it around my right wrist. I would later learn that she communicated with her paw more than any other dog I have known. In that moment, it was either love or maybe she disapproved of the way I was driving. But whatever it was, we often traveled arm in paw throughout the rest of our time together.

Definitely Not Lassie

In my pre-teenage years, I often paid after-school visits to the home of my friend David. On one memorable day, as was often the case, I was greeted at the door by his dad. But today, something felt a little different. As we entered the foyer, he stopped and said, "Parents hope for their kids to be like Mozart or Thomas Edison, or maybe Eleanor Roosevelt…" And then his voice trailed off as he motioned toward the living room. There, on the couch, was David's 6-year-old brother, Gary, flailing about like a flounder on summer pavement as he practiced his *Artificial Fart Under the Arm* trick.

I didn't dare comment. In fact, I thought Gary was doing a respectable imitation, and I was willing to bet he'd be a lot more fun at parties than Eleanor Roosevelt. Instead, I shook my head in appropriate disgust, shrugged my shoulders and trundled off to hang out with David.

As Pepper and I entered my home for the first time, I was about to gain a much better understanding of what David's dad had expressed all those years ago. Visions of spectacular greatness danced through my mind. Yes, my diamond in the rough was about to begin a journey that would make Lassie look like an also-ran.

I immediately brought her to the back yard — best to show her where she'd be "doing her business" as soon as possible. With that accomplished, I delighted in seeing her run purely for the sake of running, only stopping to flip over on her back for wriggle moments. A few minutes later, the UPS truck pulled up to the house. Since I had ordered dog toys from Amazon, I left the yard, closed the sliding screen door behind me, and headed off to collect her goodies.

Imagine my surprise when, a few seconds later, Pepper was charging through the house toward the front door. Imagine my even greater surprise when I discovered she had calculated that the shortest distance from the back yard to the front door was *through* the *closed* screen door. My fixation on the damaged screen was interrupted when I heard a commotion that eclipsed the 20 Paws of Mayhem greeting I had received at Jan's house a year earlier. There at the front door was Pepper, snarling, growling, lunging, hyperventilating, and barking, while spinning in circles like a tornado on amphetamines. Evidently, she had either invested in FedEx stock, or she simply didn't like guys in UPS uniforms. Through the blinds, I frantically motioned for the driver to just drop the box at the door. Pepper, being helpful, offered to make my communication efforts more visible by attempting to tear down the blinds.

Perhaps I was mistaken, but I couldn't recall a time when Lassie offered to help Timmy in the manner that Pepper had assisted me. Maybe those moments were in the show's outtake archives.

Rather than retrieving the package, figuring nothing builds an appetite quite like a bout of profound insanity, I began to prepare Pepper's dinner. Earlier that day, I had purchased the food she was being fed at the shelter, as well as turkey, salmon, and chicken. Once mixed together to the perfect glop consistency, with a flourish I placed the bowl on the floor, feeling like a proud French chef, and announced, "Madame, le diner est servi." Pepper approached, sniffed, sniffed again, and walked away.

Part of Great Tails' legendary lore is a story about Pepper's consumption of a live rat, which she caught while running free one evening on the grounds. In the words of Louise:

The day she caught the rat, no one knew why she was acting so skittish on the walk back. When Matt saw she had a rat, he was smart and just let her have it in her kennel. She loved eating that rat, and it amazed me that everyone was skeeved by it. What, did they think that she ordered Mexican food herself, and that was her instinct?

In fact, Matt did try to convince Pepper to surrender her catch. Once she was in her kennel, he ran to the shelter's food supply to get some chicken. Upon returning, before he had a chance to offer it for trade, Pepper looked at him, and from a front-row seat, Matt watched the rat being swallowed. While there's no accounting for tastes, I'm sure this event didn't exactly do wonders to improve Pepper's reputation at the shelter.

"You ate a rat!" I reminded her as she walked away from the savory meal I had prepared for her. "You ate a rat, and this isn't good enough for you?" Not to be defeated, I retrieved the box of animal crackers we had been munching on during the ride home. I broke a few apart and strategically placed them in the bowl, within the glop — still, no sale. In pitiful desperation, I resorted to grating the animal crackers as a garnish of sorts, to no avail.

I am unsure of how I stumbled upon it, but I discovered that if I placed her food bowl on the deck outside the back door, she'd eat her meal. My intuitive understanding of what motivated her was something that would crop up many times during our lives together. From the moment we met, we shared a bond that exceeded what was visible, or even understandable.

Thankfully, the next few hours were uneventful. Before turning in for the night, I opened what used to be my screen door so that she could go out and pee before bedtime. After a few minutes, I called her, but she didn't respond. The darkness of the yard made it difficult to locate a mostly black dog. With panic setting in, I repeatedly called and searched for her until I was interrupted by the ringing of my doorbell. A neighbor was at the front door. "Do you own a black dog? I just saw one come through the fence in your yard. She ran that way."

Fearing the worst, I ran, calling her name. I spotted her a few feet from the corner. Since dogs are wired to chase, when she looked at me, I counter-intuitively raced in the opposite direction, away from her. Within no time, a blur of black fur zipped past me. I yelled to my neighbor, who was now on my front lawn, "OPEN THE DOOR FOR HER!" As he did, Pepper barreled through. When I arrived, huffing, puffing, and choking like a 1972 Dodge Dart in need of a tune-up, I was greeted by a matter-of-fact, calm dog who looked as if she had just been napping. "ARE YOU NUTS?!" I bellowed, without a need for an answer to my question.

The first home visit. Later that evening she would escape via the small gap highlighted in the circle.

I grumbled past her and out the back door to search for the breach in the fence. In the dark, it was impossible to find. My mission was made easier when Pepper made her way through the now easy-access screen door, directly to the spot through which she had escaped. And she tried again! Reaching into the bushes while being skewered by branches, I grabbed her by the hips and pulled, thwarting the sequel to the Great Escape.

Not knowing what to expect for the rest of the evening, I attached two leashes together, fastened one end to her collar, and wrapped the other end around my wrist. That's how we slept the first night.

I can recount our first day together with humor and a warmth in my heart, mostly because in the coming months we worked our tails off adjusting Pepper's view of the world. That said, I can assure you that lying awake with her tethered to me, unsure of the future, I felt a deep level of concern. Given the issues I had seen at the shelter, my concerns about the responsibilities of dog ownership, and now her debut performance in my home, I was worried about what our future might look like. But difficult times should strengthen the love between friends more than the easy times. While watching her sleep peacefully, my concerns were transformed into a sense of purpose, framed in love. I eventually drifted off to sleep.

Author's note: Through the years I derived great pleasure, comfort, and a sense of the world being OK whenever I observed Pepper sleeping. One day while doing so, through the eyes of a parent I jotted down thoughts that came to mind. From there, I wrote and recorded a lullaby called "Come What May," which I dedicated to my goddaughter Allie for her first birthday.

"Come What May"

Sweet child, gently sleep
Let your soul take flight
Sleep child, through the night
I'll be by your side
Close your eyes, wonders await you when you rise

Come what may, I'll be there each day
To treasure every step I proudly take by your side
Come what may, hand in hand along the way
I'll always stand by you, come what may

Sweet child have no fear
I'll watch over you
Sleep child, love's embrace
will keep you all night through
Close your eyes, wonders await you when you rise

Come what may, your trust I won't betray
Your path is yours, I only hope to guide along the way
Come what may, together we will stay
I'll always stand by you, come what may
Close your eyes, wonders await you when you rise

Come what may, I'll be there each day
When the trials of life test us both, my faith in you won't stray
Come what may, together we will stay
I'll always be your home
Come what may

Orville, Wilbur, David, and My Mother

The day after Pepper baptized my home, we were scheduled to entertain visitors — my family. In advance, I had provided everyone with detailed greeting instructions, but my mother, ignoring them, set Pepper off. As she walked past a lunging, barking Pepper, she muttered, "This is as good an idea as that kite thing when you were a kid."

As an 8-year-old, I set out to establish the duration record for keeping a kite in flight. To this day, I have no idea how I would have known what that record was. It's not as if I could have Googled it, and I'm quite sure that my mother would have smelled something "rotten in Denmark" if I had asked her to drive me to the library to do some research. Perhaps I was thinking that since no established record had been documented, whatever duration I achieved *would be* the record. I'm equally unsure how I would have proven the duration of my flight. But, when a man is on a mission, even if that man is 8 years old, there's no stopping him.

I enlisted my friend David as my assistant. Orville had Wilbur; I had David. Early one evening, I launched a red, white, and blue striped kite from my back yard. David was strategically positioned in Mission Control, aka my bedroom, so that I could hand him the end of the kite string through the window. With that accomplished, I dashed into the house and tied the end of the string to my bed. The kite needed to be secured to something while, dreaming of the accolades that awaited me, I'd be peacefully sleeping through the night. I then closed the window — at the exact moment that the kite nosedived. I hurriedly reopened the window and hopelessly tried to right its course. Within seconds, seemingly the entire neighborhood was connected with kite string. TV antennas were connected to car antennas, which were connected to trees and our next-door neighbor Ben's pigeon coop. Clearly, something had been overlooked during the planning stages, like my not having a functioning brain. I considered cutting the string and tossing it over the fence to make it appear that the flight didn't originate from my yard, but I feared David would shift from Wilbur to Witness. Instead, I trundled down the hall and with appropriate contrition, fessed up to my mother. I honestly don't recall what happened next — that's probably a good thing.

Upon meeting Pepper, my mom had dredged up my *one* childhood indiscretion, implying that somehow my adoption of Pepper was equally injudicious as "that kite thing." While she may have been less than happy with the greeting she had just received, she had played a role in Pepper's outburst.

An email I sent to Mira the next morning spelled out what happened.

I instructed my sister and brother-in-law, "Call me when you're down the block and, whatever you do, don't look at us while you walk into the house." Pepper and I were already out on the lawn waiting. She got a tiny bit worked up when she saw them pull into the driveway but I kept clicking and feeding every time she looked in their direction. It worked to perfection — science usually does.

After I had given her the same exact instructions, here comes my mom up the walk, WAVING. Pepper lost it. She was barking, snarling, and lunging toward my mom, even though we were 15-20 feet away from her.

Undaunted by our rocky start, with Pepper leashed to me I sat on the couch, and using the same approach I had utilized for coaching her to make eye contact with me, clicked my clicker and treated each time she looked at a family member. The goal was for Pepper to associate, "Every time I look at someone, they somehow make the clicker go off and I get a treat. I like looking at these people. They're pretty OK after all." In doing so, Pepper's negative conditioned emotional response to strangers would hopefully be changed to a positive one.

Aside from another outburst directed at the guy my mother was dating (evidently Pepper was a good judge of character, as he turned out to be a prize jerk) she was great for the rest of the night, even falling asleep by the dining room table while we ate dinner. My sister, Gina, was the first one to ask to pet her that night. Pepper soaked up every second of it. Perhaps her affection for my sister through the years was directly tied to the fact that, after me, Gina was the first one to trust Pepper in her new world. Despite being aware of Pepper's history and having witnessed her outbursts that evening, Gina intuitively trusted her. Much the same as I had, in Pepper she saw a dog that many others didn't — a sweet, gentle soul whom she simply couldn't resist. "That face, how could anyone resist that face?" she would often ask through the years. As always, once a person respected and embraced her, Pepper welcomed them into her life. Gina became the charter member of Pepper's new inner circle. And once you were part of the inner circle, you remained there forever.

Author's note: For the rest of Pepper's life, armed with treats we greeted all first-time visitors outside the house. Her improvement was nothing short of astonishing. That said, her reaction to a stranger appearing at our door remained the same — hellacious. We continued to work on this, as it was always my goal to help Pepper change her perception of stimuli that upset her, rather than forcing her to comply with my edicts and obedience "commands." I wanted her to be comfortable and emotionally stable, much more than obedient.

Author's second note: The record for kite flying duration is 180 hours and 17 minutes, set by the Edmunds Community College kite flying team from August 21 to 29, 1982. However, I'm pretty sure I hold the record for most items connected by kite string, and unlike the Edmunds team, I achieved that virtually without assistance.

When a Freak Show Is a Good Thing

The next day was another big one in our lives — Mira and Pepper were to meet. The short drive to Mira's home was surprisingly nerve-racking — I very much wanted, and maybe even needed, her approval and was unsure how Pepper would behave. Since Mira understood dogs and their body language, Pepper quickly enrolled Mira into her new inner circle of friends. For years, in a way that was truly heart-warming, Mira affectionately referred to Pepper as "Freak Show" and "My Girl."

While "freak show" might seem similar to the "screw loose" label, given their originators, they couldn't have been more different. Mira's nickname was one of fondness, but it still acknowledged that Pepper had issues. From Mira's perspective, with work each one of those issues could be modified and even resolved. While never trivializing Pepper's behavioral quirks, the "Freak Show" moniker was a light-hearted term of affection and was spoken in a way that inspired optimism in me. On the other hand, the "screw loose" label was anything but a term of endearment, and had been glued to Pepper as an unalterable aspect of who she was, the same as her sex or coat color.

As well as the day went, it didn't occur without a hitch. After they had spent some time together, Mira reached to pet Pepper and was met with disapproval, as Pepper expressed herself by getting a bit mouthy. That evening, I emailed Mira noting that I was concerned about Pepper's response to her. Mira replied:

I'm not worried about the lippy action. Remember, fight or flight. Flight was not an option, and she was really appropriate in telling me it wasn't cool. I gave her a soft touch, and she gave me a soft lip. She matched my intensity — I think that is critical to note. I'd be more worried if I gave her a soft touch and she gave me a hard bite. That would really worry me. Instead of working on stopping the warnings (it is really all she has to communicate with), we need to desensitize her to touch, then the warnings will go away by themselves.

For a novice trainer (and equally novice dog parent) this information not only provided me with insights, but also a sense of calm and hopefulness. Over the next few months, each time I felt I was about to melt down in the face of Pepper's troubling behaviors, Mira would be there to re-energize me and provide guidance. In much the same way that Mira was my guardian angel in tough moments, during trying times in Pepper's own life, her guardian angels also appeared. From Great Tails' rescue and subsequent medical care to the small group at the shelter who kept her afloat, and from Mira's guidance in those first months to the veterinary help Pepper would receive later in her life, she and I were truly blessed at the most opportune moments.

St. Thomas Aquinas expounded, "From the very moment of his birth man has an angel guardian appointed to him." He was almost correct. Pepper and I had *several* such guardians.

"Whatever Happens, You'll Always Come First"

The Academy of Country Music (ACM) Awards ceremony is quite a prestigious event. In large part, the organization has fulfilled its goal of increasing country music's cultural presence through the airing of the show, first broadcast in 1965. In 2009, I was invited to attend the ACM Awards show. A song I had written, "It Won't Be Christmas Without You", captured the attention of some Nashville music publishers who requested a meeting with me. Clearly, this was a great opportunity, but attending meant I wouldn't be seeing Pepper while I was away. At this point she had spent four consecutive weekends visiting my house, and I had visited her every day at the shelter for well over a month, but I hadn't formally adopted her yet. Considering that the trip might help to improve my financial health, I accepted the invitation. I let Pepper know she wouldn't see me for a few days because I would be trying to make our future lives better. To ease my worries, I asked a few shelter workers to keep an eye on her. In the hopes of keeping myself close, I placed one of my t-shirts in her kennel.

The second I boarded the plane, I was broadsided by regret. I visualized Pepper sitting in her kennel looking toward the parking lot for my car, feeling that yet another person had abandoned her. From Las Vegas, I called the shelter to inform them I would be adopting her upon my return. The meetings with the publishers were no longer important. The only thing that mattered was getting back to New York and embarking on a new journey. And so, I headed home early. My life had officially gone to the dog. It would not be Christmas, or any other day, without her.

The morning after my late-night arrival from Vegas, I awoke and headed directly to Great Tails. Overwhelmed with happiness while standing in the main office completing some adoption forms, I was thinking about Pepper and how much her life was about to change. After I completed the last form, the shelter administrator inquired, "Have you seen her discharge note?" In fact, I didn't even know what a discharge note was. I smiled as I thought to myself that given her reputation, Pepper likely wasn't going to be receiving an *honorable* discharge. As I shook my head "no," I was handed a veterinarian's letter that read:

Congratulations on the adoption of your new pet! Pepper arrived at the shelter in November of 2007. She is an older female who was heartworm positive and treated appropriately. She continues to receive monthly heartworm pills. She was also diagnosed with hepatitis (inflammation of the liver) of unknown etiology. Once her medication (steroids, antibiotics, liver supplements) were started, she did well. We don't know what the future holds for Pepper. However, for the rest of her life, she will need to stay on liver supplements and will require regular blood tests.

I can still feel the gut punch. *Hepatitis... We don't know what the future holds for Pepper. Hepatitis... We don't know what the future holds for Pepper. Hepatitis... We don't know what the future holds for Pepper.* Why hadn't I been previously informed? The shockingly awful news would not dissuade me, but this wasn't the night to begin our new life. I needed to clear my head, and wanted to be 100% upbeat, positive, and reflecting nothing but pure bliss when we embarked on our journey. Pepper deserved that. And so, in a deep, swirling emotional fog, I departed the shelter without her.

Back home, I spent the evening researching Pepper's disease. I learned that there was a difference between chronic and acute hepatitis. With chronic hepatitis, the prognosis is influenced by the symptoms the dog is exhibiting at the time the disease is diagnosed, and by how much damage has been done. In other words, early detection is critical. In contrast, acute hepatitis is a short-term malady, which in some cases can be cured. In both cases, there was cause for concern.

At 8 AM the next day I spoke with the shelter's veterinarian. In the end, I was given no assurances of anything, including how long Pepper might live. Despite the awfulness of the situation, my desire to adopt her never waned. No doubt, I was concerned about my ability to navigate the waters ahead. What if she became ill? How would I take care of her while holding a full-time job? How could I live day-to-day with this hanging over our heads? My dad's words, "You'll figure it out," echoed and provided comfort as, for the last time, I drove to Great Tails to bring Pepper home.

Adoption day. Our last time at the shelter.

A few hours later in my doorway I knelt in front of Pepper and said, "Whatever happens, you'll always come first. That's a promise." And with that, we were reborn into a new life.

In the years that followed, when people questioned my relationship with her, my level of commitment, or the degree to which I structured my life around her, I'd simply respond, "I made her a promise," and leave it at that. I suppose the manner in which I spoke those words said all that needed to be said — there was never a follow-up question.

A Pain in the…Knee

"How long have you had this pain?" the doctor inquired. "About six weeks" I replied. "Well, your MRI shows a significant tear in the meniscus. You must have a very high pain tolerance. You're in need of surgery."

Later that day, I emailed Mira.

Six or so weeks ago, Pepper flipped out during a walk because a UPS truck was nearby. She lunged…slammed into my knee…ya know, the usual Pepper stuff. But this time, she hit me with such force that I actually went down in the street.

My knee has been hurting since then. It takes a lot to get me to the doctor, but I went. In fact, the cartilage is torn and I need surgery.

But hey, she's much better around the UPS truck now. That said, I'm now the one who flips out when I see a UPS truck!

Mira responded with typical, witty sarcasm:

Maybe she's better since slamming into your knee was a positive punisher (positive since you "added it" to the mix and punisher since doing so decreased the behavior of lunging). You still have another knee to use for mail carrier exercises.

Highly effective dog training, matey!

Author's note: *Positive punishment* is a concept outlined in B. F. Skinner's theory of operant conditioning. *Positive punishment* occurs when an unpleasant event is presented as the consequence of an unwanted behavior, making the unwanted behavior less likely to occur again. For example, let's say, hypothetically, while sitting in my weekly Catechism class at the age of 9, the teacher noticed that I had written "Joe Pepitone 25" (the name of my favorite sports hero, and his Yankee number) on the outside cover of my notebook. After whacking my hand with a pointing stick, she admonished me for doing so and ordered me to replace the notebook. Consequently, the behavior of me writing Joe's name on the outside cover of my new notebook was less likely to occur. Fortunately, she never looked at the *back* cover of my new notebook where, even after the knuckle-whacking, I had written his name. In Skinner's theory, the word *positive* only means that something is *added* (the whack with the pointer) as a punishment and is not to be confused with something good (positive) happening.

One week after the appointment with my doctor, I arrived at the hospital, scheduled for knee surgery. Having witnessed people speaking and acting like certified lunatics in post-surgery recovery rooms, I was resolved to not do likewise during my post-op recovery time. I'd be sure to be composed, with my wits about me, before speaking.

"Would it matter if I told you I had a big breakfast this morning?" I nervously joked as I was about to be put under general anesthesia. When I awoke, I checked the wall clock in the recovery room. It was 10:45. I dozed off, and when I again awoke, I noted it was 11:05. Aware that 20 minutes had passed, I figured I was ready to speak with lucidity. "Where are my hospital shorts?" I asked. The nurse, while laughing and dropping her head into her hands, replied, "If you ask one more time about those shorts, I swear I'm going to hit you on your knee." A few minutes later the doctor entered. "How's the comedian? Does he still want to know about his piano playing?" Evidently, I had gone vaudeville on everyone, asking, "When I go home, will I be able to play the piano?" Each time I was reassured, I replied, "Well, that's odd because

I couldn't play the piano when I arrived here this morning." So much for my plan to not speak like a certified lunatic while in recovery.

After gaining a semblance of coherence, with the doctor's order to "do something positive for yourself," I was released into the custody of my sister, who drove me home. When we arrived, I received a warm greeting from Pepper. By now, I guess I was old hat. As opposed to the days when she'd go bonkers with exuberant greetings for me, lately she was generally understated with her salutations. My sister asked, "If I leave, are you going to behave yourself?" I suppose I had raised some doubts when, exiting the car, in a show of rebellious defiance (and glorious stupidity) I had thrown my crutches across the lawn. I replied that I'd be fine and that I had no plans to go tap dancing. I thanked her for helping me and informed her that she had nothing to worry about.

Adhering to the doctor's orders to do something positive for myself, as my sister drove away, I peeked through the blinds. When she was out of sight, I grabbed Pepper's leash, retrieved one crutch from the front lawn, and hobbling, escorted her for a walk. What could be more positive than walking one's dog?

Perhaps, if I had owned a piano, I would have busied myself there but as my surgeon, and everyone else who had spoken with me that morning had learned, I didn't. It was such a beautiful day for a walk — and we had a lot of training work to do.

A Truckload of Challenges

My surgery highlighted the undeniable fact that Pepper and I needed to work on her reactivity to delivery trucks. When it came to behavior modification, the methodology I often used with Pepper was rooted in *Pavlovian conditioning*. In the early 1900s, Ivan Pavlov, a Russian scientist, set out to demonstrate that dogs have hard-wired, unconditioned responses to certain stimuli, such as salivating over food, an unconditioned stimulus. While engaged in his work, Pavlov stumbled upon an unexpected discovery — dogs would salivate not only over food, which he had expected, but also over stimuli that portended food was about to be served, such as a lab assistant entering the room to feed the dogs. In order to test his discovery, just prior to feeding his laboratory dogs, Pavlov rang a bell. In short order, whenever the bell (a previously neutral stimulus) was rung, the dogs would salivate in anticipation of being fed. In Pepper's case, the challenge was more difficult, as her response to the stimulus, in this case trucks, wasn't neutral. It was negative.

The plan for modifying her delivery truck reactivity was similar to a Pavlovian protocol we had already successfully utilized to reduce her extreme reactions to garbage trucks arriving at our home. Three times each week at 6:15 AM, garbage trucks made pick-ups. On those mornings, I positioned myself near the front door awaiting the truck's arrival. The moment Pepper heard the "beep" of the truck, I started feeding her great food. All her favorites, except a live rat, were on the menu. The goal was to "pin" the response she had to foods she loved, "OH BOY!" to the stimulus, in this case the "beep" of the garbage truck. In fairly short order, her conditioned response to the "beep" became, "OH BOY! A GARBAGE TRUCK!" — just like when Pavlov's dogs heard his bell ringing. When the truck departed, all feeding stopped: "BUMMER. I HATE WHEN THE TRUCK LEAVES." Once she started to exhibit a positive anticipation after hearing the truck's "beep" (her ears would perk up and she'd look toward my treat-paying hand), I knew the "beep" had taken on a new meaning. The next step was to position myself a bit farther from her so she'd have to leave the front door to collect her food. Within a fairly short time, she'd hear the truck's "beep" and come running to me for her great food reward. After that, I added a "sit" cue before paying her. From that moment on, unprompted by me, whenever she heard the garbage truck she'd come to me, sit, and get a treat. Problem solved. Underlying emotions and reaction changed.

Developing a similar response to encounters with delivery trucks, specifically UPS trucks, proved to be much more challenging. UPS truck arrival times were not predictable and were not announced with a "beep" — a very clear and easy stimulus with which to work. Additionally, the arrival of the truck was a predictor of something Pepper truly disliked — a person wearing a uniform coming to our front door to ring the doorbell. Her reactivity was so powerful that not only had she sent me for surgery after seeing a UPS truck on the street (a less highly charged context than the front door) but in another incident, she caused me even greater pain. As per usual, I reached out to Mira:

Hey. Pepper bit me. I'm pretty much in shock.

Took her out back where we played for a half hour. Then we went for a drive (she loves that)...came back and the UPS truck was on my block...we stood by my front door, waiting...he pulled up a few houses away, she spotted the truck and went ballistic...she was calm for a half second...I reached to pet her and she went into another frenzy and bit me, twice. She didn't break skin but left marks...It was a "get your hand away from me" kind of bite...quick, twice...no blood, no holding on or anything like that.

And unfortunately, in total shock, I reacted by sorta slapping her on the top of her head…not at all hard…it was reflexive…yet horrible. I am extremely upset.

Mira was swift with her response:

Quick observations:

Context-specific — on property different than off property. Makes it fall into the predictable category.

Reactivity crosses over into frustration and displaced aggression. However, the threshold has been high, since she hasn't done this until now.

She bites (duh, I coulda told ya that one) but it was inhibited. She would have taken your hand off if it wasn't. That's much better than a dog that doesn't bite but has no bite inhibition, until one day, uh oh!! Those three things make for a good prognosis — predictable, high threshold, bite inhibition.

You reacted — you didn't beat her to a pulp. You inhibited yourself and have a high threshold. You're made for each other :)

Now get back to work, you have several thousand more reps to go…

Once again, Mira's guardianship could have easily rivaled that of Clarence from the classic *It's a Wonderful Life*. Pepper and I didn't perform the prescribed several thousand reps, but we worked with extreme dedication and made great strides. Upon seeing UPS trucks during our walks, she'd still get a bit frantic but would always look to me for a treat. With that, her focus was off the truck, which was always a good thing.

UPS trucks arriving at our home presented a vastly different challenge. With an eye toward increasing training opportunities, I began ordering home deliveries of every imaginable item from Amazon. Toothpaste. Plastic cups.

Bottled water. Scones (scones?). But until her last day, Pepper remained reactive. To better manage her behavior, we established a cue called "Party Time." Just as Pavlov's dogs were conditioned to expect food after hearing the ringing of a bell, Pepper learned that "Party Time" was a predictor of great food. I conditioned the cue by saying it and then following it with a food orgy tossed on the floor. Repeat and repeat. She quickly learned that "party time" was just that. In mid-outburst, she'd hear the cue and come running to collect her pay, leaving the UPS truck behind.

I didn't spend time trying to figure out why Pepper viewed UPS trucks and their drivers with such acrimony. Even if I had uncovered the roots, her response wouldn't have changed. I suspect that my inability to successfully change her response was in part linked to self-reinforcing behavior, i.e., "I bark and the truck leaves. Ah, that feels better." She had plenty of opportunities to practice this whenever I wasn't home, and each time she did, the reactivity became more deeply imprinted.

Or it could have been that she was just being Pepper. Dogs, just like humans, are individuals with different — and sometimes irrational — likes and dislikes. I don't like mustard. I've never even *tried* mustard, but I'm *sure* I don't like it. In fact, I don't even like being in the same room as mustard. And, I'd appreciate it if no one tried to change my mind about it. Much as I would have preferred a different response from Pepper, I eventually accepted her animosity toward the UPS driver — just as without trying to change me, she accepted my intense loathing for the odious demon, mustard.

Thunder Phobia

Sniff, sniff. Snort. Huff. Snort, sniff. The sounds were coming from the living room. Pepper agitatedly paced between the window and the front door, sniffing at the base of each. Assuming she had identified something outside, I opened the front door expecting her to react. Instead, she ran to a different window and began sniffing there, only stopping to manically dig at the carpet. Something was dramatically wrong.

As the skies darkened and Pepper's behavior became more frantic, the puzzle was easily solved — my newly adopted dog was thunder phobic. Frenetically moving from room to room, her fears escalated with each passing minute. Back in the living room, she knocked over a lamp while desperately attempting to hide behind a chair. Saliva ran from her mouth. Her body trembled. Her pupils dilated. And her breathing was coming in short bursts. I feared she would suffer a heart attack.

No amount of consoling or attempts at comforting her proved helpful. In fact, I couldn't get her to stay in one place long enough to provide support. As the thunder bellowed, hoping to drown out the sound, I blasted the stereo at a concert-level volume. I also turned on the washing machine and dishwasher. But nothing was working. Finally, about 45 minutes later she calmed down. With the noise level in the house rivaling that of a Manhattan subway station at rush hour, I was unsure if the storm had passed. I called my sister, who lived just a few minutes away, for a weather report. The storm had passed.

During the next month, I tried everything to help Pepper — thunder capes, calming scents like dog appeasing pheromones and lavender, pink light, Rescue Remedy, binaural music, and black-out shades for the windows. Due to her liver condition, I was very hesitant to use any medications but, despite this, on two separate occasions I gave her drugs —alprazolam once and Benadryl another time. Nothing worked. But, we didn't give up.

Determined to not allow her to suffer, I devised an effective protocol. A few years later, I shared it through *The APDT Chronicle of the Dog* training magazine, the largest circulation magazine written by and for positive-reinforcement trainers.

The Bunker Protocol
Chronicle of the Dog, September 2012

Thunderstorm season has arrived. For dog owners who live with a thunder-phobic pooch, it's a time of year that can be particularly trying — for the dog, it's downright awful.

I am one of those dog owners. At one time, I loved thunderstorms. Three years ago, I adopted my rescue, Pepper. Since then, my love for storms has waned and summers have become an emotional roller coaster ride.

To a great extent, my life has been controlled by the whim of the weather. Beginning with the arrival of spring and lasting through early fall, I am acutely aware of the weather forecast for each upcoming week. I react with an elevated heart rate each time I see a weather icon depicting clouds, rain, and a lightning bolt.

Although every storm provides an opportunity for me to work on behavior modification with my dog, and even though her thunderstorm phobia has become more manageable, perhaps because of that work, I don't welcome the arrival of storms.

The experience for the average dog owner, who is not a trainer, is surely considerably worse. The following article focuses on the thunderstorm management plan I developed for Pepper. I don't represent this plan as anything but what it is: a management plan. Additionally, I don't suggest that what I've created is a cure-all or that the plan is even scientifically valid. I don't characterize this as a new breakthrough to an old, intractable problem.

But I do represent this as a procedure that seemingly has provided me with sufficient upside that I can work on counter-conditioning my dog during storms. Prior to creating the plan, this wasn't possible.

At minimum, if I can prevent my dog's phobia from tracking the typical curve, that is, worsening with age, I'll be thrilled. I am hopeful that sharing this plan will spark thought and the exchange of ideas, and maybe even serve as a catalyst for the creation of similar, more effective plans.

As thunderstorm phobia is extremely resistant to counter-conditioning, management of the dog's reactivity is most often utilized instead. Unlike other easily mimicked auditory stimuli that cause phobic responses in dogs (such as fireworks, trucks, landscaping equipment, etc.) thunder phobia differs in that the afflicted dog often reacts to a suite of conditioned stimuli that precede and serve as predictors of the impending storm. Changes in ozone levels, falling barometric pressure, static electricity, wind patterns, and rain are a few examples of conditioned stimuli to which the thunder-phobic dog might respond. These triggers are impossible, or nearly impossible, to recreate for the purpose of counter-conditioning. Additionally, during storms the phobic dog experiences a physiological reaction to storm-related stimuli that makes counter-conditioning exceedingly difficult.

The dog's initial assessment of the storm-predicting stimuli happens very quickly, and reactivity rapidly ratchets up to full strength as sensory input (ozone, barometric pressure, etc.) is received. In other words, thunder-phobic dogs react; they don't think. Once this process is initiated, hormones release into the system that prepare the dog for an energetic reaction, more commonly referred to as "fight or flight."

My initial goal with Pepper was to prevent/offset the ramping up of fear so that her physical/emotional/physiological state, while not optimal, wouldn't be entirely counter-productive to counter-conditioning. To that end, I decided to create a protocol that would quickly, powerfully, and positively engage all of her senses. My hope was that once she developed a +CER (positive conditioned emotional response) to the protocol, when presented during a storm, it might help to counterbalance her thunderstorm fear before it became a full-blown phobic episode.

My tools:

- *A hair scrunchie*
- *A lavender scented candle*
- *White noise machine*
- *CD of soft music*
- *VERY high-value food*

We began by practicing the plan only during nice weather. In my office (the windows were fitted with blackout shades to prevent her from seeing lightning flashes when we went "live" with the plan) the candle was lit, music played, and the white noise machine was switched on.

Outside the office, I placed the scrunchie high up on Pepper's leg, where her leg meets her body. I called out "bunker" in a happy voice and ran to the office with her. Once there, I cued her to go to her bed.

While on her bed, she was massaged and continually provided with treats. After 5-7 minutes, we stopped and returned to regular life. (Note: the purpose of the scrunchie was to engage her body in a unique way that predicted the wonderful stuff that was coming. I could have used any one of a number of items, but the scrunchie seemed perfect for the procedure. I used the lavender candle because lavender is a calming scent; white noise would serve to block out sound; soft music has been shown to have a calming effect. My goal was to engage all senses and to create a +CER to the word "Bunker."

After a dozen repetitions of the plan, the mere mention of the word "bunker" would induce a happy dance that rivaled any that Snoopy ever performed. We were ready to go live.

At the onset of the next storm, with the first sign of reactivity on her part, I immediately prepared the room, placed the scrunchie on her leg, called out "bunker" and went to the office with her. She was still afraid (panting, salivating, trembling) and was not interested in food, but she wasn't performing any of the old behaviors, such as clawing at the baseboards, digging at the carpet, running through the house, pacing frantically, etc. We rode the storm out on her bed: a significant improvement.

After approximately eight weeks and several storms, I went to bed one night aware of early-morning storms in the forecast. I had prepared for the storm by assembling all the "Bunker" items. That night, I was awakened by Pepper tapping on my shoulder with her paw as if to say, "Hey, storm! Bunker. Let's go." When I arose from bed, she ran ahead of me to the office. There was no need to call out "Bunker." Had the storm become a CS (conditioned stimulus) for a new CR (conditioned response)? If so, this was another noteworthy occurrence.

I continued working the Bunker protocol with Pepper with some fascinating results. She will now accept food during thunderstorms, which presents me with the opportunity to counter-condition during real storms. Rather than only linking food presentation with stimuli that I perceive (thunder and lightning). I do so each time she shows any sign of fear. I fully believe that she is responding to more than I can perceive, and I "pay" accordingly.

She is now able to endure storms outside of my office in a few safe zones (selected by her) we utilize. On occasion, we practice the Bunker routine, but we haven't used it during a live storm in a while. I have noticed she triggers a bit earlier and to more subtle weather changes, but her reaction to storms isn't remotely as powerful as it once was. Without having any accurate ways to measure (other than her willingness to accept food and a reduction in phobic behavior, which are both significant developments), I would classify her current reaction to storms as being fearful but not phobic. That she now accepts food during storms provides me with a chance to counter-condition her reactivity/fear. And therein lies my hope for the future.

Perhaps Pepper's improvement is coincidental and is linked to something other than the Bunker protocol. Perhaps what I'm seeing as improvement actually isn't. There are far too many variables for me to directly connect any behavioral changes to the Bunker routine. But if nothing else, the protocol has provided me with a reason to remain inspired and creative in the hopes that we can turn her phobia into a thing of the past.

The specifics of the Bunker protocol aren't important. The scrunchie could be replaced with a thunder shirt; the lavender scent could be replaced with a DAP diffuser or spray (so long as it is only used during the protocol). The particulars are less important than the goal: creating a +CER that engages all senses, which can perhaps be used to counterbalance the ramping up of fear.

It is often stated that thunderstorm phobia in dogs is an intractable malady with next to no chance of being altered; perhaps so. Hopefully, for the afflicted dogs and their distressed owners, we will be equally obstinate in our dedication and desire to overcome, or at least abate, the impact of thunderstorm reactivity in our canine friends.

During the nine summers that we lived together, Pepper was never without me during a thunderstorm. If I had scheduled a business appointment, I canceled it. Social functions took second place. Once, I bailed mid-dinner with my friend and trainer extraordinaire, Dr. Ian Dunbar, and rushed home when a thunderstorm popped up unexpectedly. In fact, Ian knew me well enough to say, "OK. Time for you to go," the moment we heard the very distant rumbling. Fortunately, a family wedding, graduation, birthday party, or funeral never occurred during a thunderstorm. If so, I would have upset more than a few people.

For years, the Bunker Protocol worked beautifully. In 2013, when we moved to North Carolina, Pepper found her comfort zone in a new bunker — a protected area by the couch in our living room. Until the last year of her life, when her health prevented her from doing so, she rode out all storms there in relative calm.

While I did all I could to help her, including becoming an expert at reading weather radar maps, each storm chipped a little piece off my heart, as I was never able to completely comfort her. I learned that, like all of us, she was on her own journey, and I could only control certain elements of her world.

It was a lesson that would repeat itself, in spades, a few years later.

Sy and Paul

The two men had met 25 years earlier as members of a running club. While time had eroded their physical skills, the bond between them remained strong. When, due to age, running together was no longer an option, they instead walked through our neighborhood. And on mornings when walking became a struggle for him, Sy, the older of the two, would lean on Paul, who supported him by his arm as they navigated their daily route.

During my initial conversation with them, I learned that Sy was one of those folks who truly believed that all dogs loved him. He wasn't the least bit dissuaded by Pepper's greeting of lunges, barks, and growls. Sy was also impervious to my requests: "Please don't reach for her. Please just stand still," I'd vainly coach whenever we encountered the two friends on their morning walk.

It didn't help that Sy wore a reflective orange vest and also hung a whistle around his neck. For most dogs, different equals dangerous. Often when encountering novel stimuli, as they fend off the perceived threat, a dog's mindset is, "I might be wrong but at least I won't be dead." People don't typically wear large, fluorescent orange vests so, for Pepper, Sy was a novel stimulus. As such, she was more than willing to express her distaste for both him and his outfit.

Given Pepper's animus for Sy, most people in my shoes would have avoided him during our walks. But my journey with Pepper was never about normalcy — it was about helping us to lead a better life, and helping her to overcome her fears. And so, we set out to do just that.

Armed with high-value treats during our walks, the moment Pepper spotted Sy and Paul, the feeding began. With each repetition, we'd get closer and closer to Sy and eventually, we built enough confidence to allow him to feed her. Within a short time, whenever Pepper saw Sy and Paul she'd begin to wag her tail, and whenever they spotted Pepper they'd cross the street to greet us. Chatting with them was always a highlight of my day. They were bright and delightfully entertaining — our conversations would often go on for as much as a half hour, with a relaxed Pepper sitting, or lying down, by my side. The guys would occasionally pet her while she reveled in the attention. Only a few months earlier, out of unfounded fear, shelter workers who *thought* they knew her had declined my invitation to pet her.

Not too long after our new friendship had been established, we bumped into Sy and Paul while on our morning walk. The usual greeting ceremony ensued and then, with a smile and a slight look of disbelief, Paul said, "Sy, take off your glove and show him your hand." Sy did so, exposing a badly bruised and bitten hand. Paul continued, "He went to pet a strange dog the other morning, and the dog bit him." Clearly, Sy needed to learn a few things from Pepper about being wary when confronting novel stimuli.

Sy (note the vest and whistle) petting Pepper while Pepper and Paul check each other out.

Later that year, since they were such an important part of Pepper's growth, and since we had both developed a warm affection for Sy and Paul, I took a picture of Pepper with the duo. In the photograph, Sy, resplendent in his bright orange vest, is seen holding Pepper's leash and petting her chest. Pepper, wearing her fur-lined, tan suede vest, is looking up at Paul, seemingly thinking, "I like you, but sometimes you're kinda big."

The following spring, the photograph of the three friends was used at the conclusion of a 20-minute webinar presented by a leader in the field of dog training, chronicling the methodology and protocols I had used to help Pepper overcome her fear of strangers. I often received credit for Pepper's transformation but always rejected it by noting that she did all the heavy lifting.

Author's note: Four years later, the day before Pepper and I were leaving New York for our move to North Carolina, weighing heavily on my mind was the awareness that sadly, we'd not be seeing Sy and Paul any longer. I didn't know how I'd say goodbye or express my appreciation for what they meant to us. On our morning walk, as Pepper and I turned the corner we saw Paul walking by himself. With a smile, I called over, "Good morning. Did Sy finally wise up and dump you?" Paul approached and with sorrow lamented, "Sy died last night."

During times like these, one becomes aware of just how inadequate words can be. Paul and I simply stood in the street, with Pepper between us, lost. I finally spoke, "Do you think you'd be able to get Sy's whistle for me? I'd like to attach it to Pepper's harness." It was all I could think to say. We hugged and walked off in different directions, never to meet again.

Hopefully, Sy had finally found a place where all dogs liked him.

A Step Away — A Step Toward

During our first months together, the training schedule with Pepper continued to be a busy one. Several behaviors, all fear-based, needed to be addressed for her to enjoy life more fully. Separation anxiety, resource guarding, body handling reactivity, aggression toward dogs during our walks, and more were on the list. Of all the issues requiring attention, addressing Pepper's separation anxiety was the most pressing.

Canine separation anxiety is a malady so challenging that even experienced, educated trainers frequently shy away from accepting these cases. Fortunately, my inexperience served me well, as I never saw the obstacles that were in plain sight for more experienced trainers.

Like most separation distressed dogs, Pepper reacted poorly to anything, such as keys being picked up, that predicted she was going to be left alone. The first order of business was to weaken her association to those triggers, or better still, turn them into positives. Once again employing methods rooted in Pavlovian conditioning, several times each day, I'd pick up my keys, toss her a treat and then place the keys back down. Any predictive trigger was handled the same way. Jacket on, treat tossed, jacket off. Shoes on, treat tossed, shoes off. During this time, I didn't leave her alone, because doing so would likely have undone our progress. When addressing behavioral issues, it's critical that the dog be kept from experiencing upset with the stimulus/context that is causing the issue. In this case, being left alone was the problem, so we avoided that. To some, suspending absences might sound like a major burden, but for me, it was easy. The prospect of Pepper being terribly upset in my absence was much worse than the alternative — staying home with her, or having someone sit with her, until she was comfortable being alone.

Within a short period of time, she began to build a positive association to each of the departure triggers. The next order of business was practicing desensitization and counter-conditioning to my absences. This was done in small, incremental steps, initially by placing her in her confinement area — a gated room on the main floor — with high-value food as I stood outside the room. Step by step, as long as she didn't display any signs of distress, I'd move closer to the front door, until I was able to stand outside my home for very short durations. From there, I'd watch her on my phone, wait until she had finished her treats so that she learned to self-soothe when treats weren't available, and then re-enter the house. I was very careful to not increase the duration of each absence, because I didn't want her to get wise to the fact that each absence was getting longer. Instead, I'd leave for one minute, then 30 seconds, then two minutes, then 45 seconds, etc.

One day, when I closed the front door behind me, I realized I had forgotten my cell phone. I waited a few minutes then re-entered to find a sleeping Pepper. She heard me, slowly rose, stretched, and greeted me at the gate. Hot diggity. Progress had been made. From that point forward, we were pretty much on our way to success. Over the years, while watching her via remote camera, it was clear she was never thrilled about being left alone, but always managed to settle down within a few minutes.

When we weren't working on her separation anxiety, Pepper's tendency to guard her resources needed to be addressed. Her most intense guarding occurred when she was in possession of high-value items, such as a bone or bully stick. This problem had first manifested when she bit me at the shelter while in possession of a pig's ear. It would have been great to use logic to solve the problem: "Look, dopey. If I wanted your bully stick, I wouldn't have given it to you in the first place." Even though training doesn't work that way, I did occasionally try to reason with her. Hey, ya never know.

Pepper's "whale eye" (a canine sign of stress, often followed by aggression) while guarding a bone.

With the separation anxiety protocol, I practiced taking small steps *away* from her, paired with great food. For modification of her guarding issues, I did the opposite. To start, while she was in possession of a low-value item, I armed myself with her favorite foods, took a step *toward* her, tossed a treat, then walked away. When she began to show happy anticipation during my approach, I took two steps toward her, tossed a treat, and retreated, then three, and so on. Once I was able to claim the item in trade, we moved up to a more valued item and repeated the entire process. I also opportunistically practiced trading up for better items any time she was in possession of a resource. Eventually, she began happily dropping whatever item was in her possession the second she saw me approach. Within a few weeks, the problem was resolved, never to resurface.

The foundation for all our work was always the same: modify the underlying emotions, rather than forcing discipline as a resolution. I was starting to feel pretty good about myself as a trainer. For each issue, I had devised a training protocol that worked. My confidence soared. I began to think that there wasn't any problem we couldn't solve. I suspect it was at this moment that the Dog Training Gods looked down on me and decided to challenge my hubris.

Car-nivorous

The words "Hey Pepps, wanna go for a ride?" were always greeted with bright eyes and a wagging tail. This time was no different. Upon opening the car door, I noticed a gash in a leather panel of my beloved Corvette. It equally sickened and puzzled me. I had no recollection of doing anything that could have caused the ugly tear. A week earlier, a friend pointed out some small teeth marks in the dashboard. Perhaps I was in denial and simply wasn't ready to add yet another item to the list of Pepper's behavioral quirks, but I chose to ignore the observation. A few days later, when I discovered a tear in the opposite door panel, I had no choice but to accept the ugly truth. Houston, we have a problem. My dog is tearing up the inside of my car.

When left alone in the car, if someone walked by, Pepper had been redirecting her stranger reactivity toward the dashboard and door panels. Despite how creative I had been with her previous training, this time I was stumped. That's not to say that I didn't come up with a nifty strategy or two, such as placing a remote-controlled treat dispenser in the car. While I was hidden from her, I could trigger it each time she saw a person. As a result, just like with the "beep" of the garbage truck, she'd build a positive association to the sighting of a person. But I nixed that plan when I realized it was dependent on the treat dispenser being in the car at all times, and that the plan would likely take an eternity before yielding any results.

In the end, I chose to restrict her opportunities to engage in the behavior by having her wear an oversized mesh muzzle while in the car. Often, limiting a dog's opportunities to practice an unwanted behavior helps to resolve the problem. No longer able to practice the old behavior, the dog replaces it with a new, and hopefully more acceptable one.

Since Pepper had been forced to wear a muzzle for all veterinary examinations during her shelter years, she wasn't exactly fond of them. And so began more desensitization and counter-conditioning. To start, I'd show her the muzzle and then give her a treat. Because I wanted to make sure she was developing a positive association to only the muzzle and nothing else, I'd also show other items and *not* give her food. In this way, I was certain she wasn't building a positive response to anything other than what I intended: the muzzle. With this accomplished, I began to give her treats *through* the muzzle. With each repetition I pulled my hand back a bit further, requiring her to push her face deeper into the muzzle to get the treat. Finally, I used the muzzle for fetch games. As with all other transformations in her emotions, seeing her new association to the muzzle, evident by a wagging tail and bright eyes, truly warmed my heart. She had learned to anticipate something good when the muzzle was in view.

For the next month, Pepper wore the over-sized mesh muzzle each time I exited the car. Since redirecting toward the door panels was no longer an option, she instead chose to lie down and fall asleep, or simply sit and watch the world go by. Confident that a new behavior had been established, I began leaving her in the car unmuzzled. I will admit to being nervous doing so after the interior of the car was fixed, but she never again engaged in the destructive behavior.

Author's note: One day, as I approached my car after exiting a Staples store, I encountered an elderly man standing beside it who commented, "I've never seen such a calm dog." "Yep. She's always been that way," I jokingly replied. But, there was truth in my comment. While I often received compliments about how I had "trained" Pepper, in fact, I had only helped her reclaim who she was prior to so many people screwing her up. All I did was peel away the unhealthy layers that others had added, or that she had added in order to survive, covering up the essence of who she was — a damn good dog.

"Work with Your Dog"

Toward the end of my first summer with Pepper, Mira mentioned that she was organizing an obedience Olympics. Pepper and I decided we should compete — a questionable decision considering we had been so busy working on behavioral stuff that obedience training had taken a decided back seat. But hey, David slew Goliath; the U.S. team beat the Russians in the "Miracle on Ice"; I graduated high school. In other words, anything can happen.

The Olympics challenges were geared for dogs who had passed Mira's intermediate level classes. While we had attended a number of those sessions, truth be told, we weren't there to learn obedience cues. Instead, we were learning how to be comfortable around strangers and other dogs. Oh, we may have *appeared* to be practicing cues, but that was just a clever disguise. While others were happily rewarding their dogs for compliance with obedience cues, Pepper was getting paid for simply looking at other dogs and people. During moments when I'd anticipate her getting upset, expecting a growl I'd warn, "If they hear you, we're gonna get tossed out of the class. Don't, don't, don't..." And Pepper, being Pepper, would grumble anyway. And I'd laugh because there was clearly a difference in her tone from her shelter days.

Mira's contest comprised three events: Sit, Recall Race, and Shape a New Behavior. For the "sit" challenge, Mira would call out for the owners to request a sit from their dogs in varying positions — owner standing, sitting, lying on the ground, standing on one leg, while walking, from 25 feet away and more. In all, there were 13 such challenges for the event. The dog needed to comply within three seconds to a single cue from the handler. For the second event, we were permitted one week to teach our dog to come on cue without the use of any hand or verbal cues. And finally, the Olympics would conclude with a "shaping" competition. Through a training technique known as shaping, competitors would be given a choice to train one of two behaviors within an allotted time of five minutes.

When asked to explain the reason behind the extraordinary success of his comedy partnership with Dean Martin, without hesitation Jerry Lewis explained that they played to each other with the hopes of getting the other guy to laugh, and there just happened to be an audience watching. Truth be told, I couldn't have cared less about our placing in the competition. I informed Pepper of this during our drive to the event: "Hey, bud, this is just for me and you. Let's go have fun." I mostly wanted to experience something new with her, and hopefully have fun while doing so.

The first day of the Olympics featured the "sit" competition. As we entered the event area, I immediately scoped out the other contestants. The field consisted of a few Goldens, Labs, one Pit Bull, and a few others. Other than breeds, I don't recall details about the other contestants except one: a Portuguese Water Dog who was behaving manically, jumping up and nipping at her owner, hanging onto a toy (front paws off the ground) and not releasing when asked to do so, and barking at other dogs. Finally, out of frustration, the owner tethered the dog to a fence post. "Well," I confidently concluded, "at least we won't finish in last place."

Once the "sit" competition began, the more I observed the dogs performing before us, the more I suspected that Pepper was going to be darn good at this. When it was her turn, she performed flawlessly on 12 of the 13 sit cues. The only one we missed was my request for Pepper to sit while walking on leash, as I kept walking. By this time, Pepper had learned to walk next to me quite well, so when I cued "sit" and kept going, she followed right along. Amazingly, after our round, we were in first place. Only one dog remained — the Portuguese Water Dog. "This is going to be fun to watch. Too bad I didn't think to bring popcorn," I thought as owner and dog approached the performance area. If I was a betting man, I would have set the over/under at two correct responses — and bet the under.

I learned a valuable lesson that day, something that I have since incorporated into my training sessions. Despite how often Mira preached it, without fading the use of food when training, there's a risk of creating a "show me the money" dog — a dog who only performs when s/he knows food is available. To my amazement, the Water Dog scored 13 out of 13. When the lights and camera were on, and food was in the offing, she did a great job. When food wasn't immediately available, her behavior fell apart.

At the end of the day, Pepper, once labeled as "untrainable" with a "screw loose" stood alone in second place. I was damn proud of her.

During the following week we practiced the second event, our new recall cue, aka coming when called. In keeping with the rules, no hand or verbal cues, I decided to use a harmonica for our cue. Multiple times each day, whenever I'd toot the harmonica something great would follow — treats offered, car rides, bully sticks, play sessions in the yard. The harmonica became a 100% predictor of great things and as such, whenever Pepper heard it, she came running, in much the same way the sound of jingling bells caused me to chase after the Good Humor truck when I was a kid.

On the day of the event, we arrived with our secret-weapon harmonica in my pocket. A race area had been established with the starting line marked by two orange cones. The finish line was 50 feet away. The challenge was straightforward: cue your dog to come with the newly learned cue, and then to sit when s/he arrived at the finish line. Two heats were allowed for each dog. The fastest of the two trials was used to determine the standings.

When our turn arrived, I called Pepper to the starting line and cued her to sit and stay. I hurriedly walked the length of the running lane to the finish line and brandished my harmonica. Fully expecting to see Pepper break the sound barrier, I sounded the cue. With the clock running, she sat motionless — stone-cold motionless. She had learned her "stay" cue so well that unless she heard the word "Release," she wasn't going to move. If there had been a "sit-stay" event, we'd have set the world record. As was often the case, I found her to be entertaining, even when things didn't work out as I had planned. The first heat was blown, but we still had one more chance.

When we were called for our second run, I set Pepper up at the starting line in a standing position, without cueing her to stay. Instead, Mira held her in place. From my position 50 feet away, I loudly tooted the harmonica. Within three steps, Pepper was at full speed. She bolted toward me in a blur. Five feet from the finish line I cued her to sit. She jammed on the brakes and sat. Mira checked her stopwatch. We were officially in first place.

Only one heat remained, and it was to be run by none other than the Portuguese Water Dog. I hadn't seen the little dog's first run, but figured she wouldn't be focused enough to make it to the finish line. Using a dog whistle, her owner cued her to come. The little dog bolted and completed the race a fraction of a second faster than Pepper. Off to the side, I sort of jokingly lobbied Judge Mira that the dog's weight should have been factored into the scoring. Pepper weighed twice as much as the Water Dog, and that should have been a consideration in the scoring. At the end of my eloquent and cogent argument, we remained in second place.

And now we readied ourselves for the final challenge: teaching a behavior through shaping. Shaping is defined as the differential reinforcement of successive approximations toward a target behavior. In a version of English that doesn't make you feel as if two monkeys are fighting over one banana inside your head, this means that you start by reinforcing small aspects of a desired behavior, and gradually build up the behavior until you reach your final goal. Think of the game "Hot and Cold." When the subject approaches the goal, we say "hot." Otherwise, we say "cold." Shaping is similar. When the dog shows progress toward the goal, we mark the behavior with a clicker, or any other positive marker, and reinforce with food. Rather than saying "cold" when the dog strays from the target behavior, we simply say nothing.

Mira offered the contestants two choices — shape our dogs to cross over a low-incline A-frame, or shape the dog to set off a Staples' "That Was Easy" button. The allotted time to shape the behavior was five minutes, after which, when called on, the dog was required to perform the newly shaped behavior within one minute. Everyone except me and Pepps chose the A-frame, which was the easier event. We were going to show the crowd just how easy "That Was Easy" could be.

During the early stages of our five-minute shaping session, anytime Pepper showed interest in the button, even if she just looked at it from 20 feet away, I clicked and treated. After that, I raised the criteria and didn't click until she made a motion toward the button. Eventually, I only clicked when she contacted it. With time to spare, she started setting the button off. Multiple "That was easy!" announcements emanating from the button were music to my ears. Each time she set it off, I'd capture the behavior by pointing and saying "button" just before she did so. In this way, the behavior was now on cue. I didn't know it then, but this ain't easy stuff to accomplish in such a short timeframe, especially with distractions like other dogs, people, scents, etc. in the vicinity. Still, I was amazed that Pepper learned it as quickly as she did. I suspect Great Tails' Matt was right when months earlier he proclaimed that she was the smartest shelter dog he had ever known.

When our five-minute learning session concluded, we moved off to the side and watched others attempt their A-frame challenge. There wasn't a lot of drama and excitement, and even less success. A few dogs got it right but most didn't seem particularly interested.

And now, it was our turn. Mira called out, "Pepper and John." With everyone watching, and my heart racing, we were ready — except we were thrown a last-second curve: I was instructed to stand behind a line and send Pepper out to set off the button, which was approximately 15 feet from where I was standing. I had expected that I'd be able to stand near the button and direct her to it, just as we had done during our learning session.

Mira declared, "One minute. Ready. Start!" With the clock ticking, Pepper was doing a fabulous job of wandering around the fenced area, sniffing where other dogs had been, and generally enjoying a leisurely tour of the entire yard. In fact, she went everywhere *except* where the button was located.

At the 30 second point, I looked at Mira and shrugged, as if to say, "Uh, this isn't going to happen." Her response was something I have never forgotten: "Work WITH your dog." It wasn't so much the words as the way she spoke them that left a lasting impression on me. Mira had reminded me that Pepper and I were a team and that, if we don't give up on them, dogs are capable of amazing things.

With a newfound determination, I tooted the harmonica to get Pepper's attention. She arrived at my side in a flash. I motioned with my hand for her to go to the other side of the yard, which she did. She was now positioned so that when I again called her, she'd need to pass the button while coming to me. This time I didn't use the harmonica to get her attention because upon hearing it, she would have bolted right past the Staples' button. Instead, I calmly called, "Pepps, come." As she made her way toward me, when approaching the button I pointed and called out, "Pepper, BUTTON!" And damn if she didn't set it off just as time was running out.

The entire audience, many of whom knew Pepper's history, erupted into applause, cheers, and laughs of pure joy. And Pepper, oh, how that dog proudly bucked, danced, and pranced around the yard. As I watched her strut her stuff, I flashed to visions of an emaciated, abandoned dog roaming the unfamiliar streets of Long Island, and to those dark 22 months of life in a cage while being demonized by many around her. I'm proud to say I did so with welled eyes.

At the close of the Olympics, when the final scores were tallied, we came in second to the Portuguese Water Dog. But we finished first in each other's hearts — and I doubt Dean Martin and Jerry Lewis ever had more fun.

Cary, North Carolina

Over the next few years, Pepper and I enjoyed the simple pleasures of a halcyon life. Our days were filled with peaceful walks during which I'd sing newly channeled songs to her, visits to a nearby lake and nature trail, trick training, car rides, and games like hide 'n' seek, tug, fetch, and "find it." We also enrolled in a few of Mira's classes, with Pepper's favorite being the low-key "Walk About," during which we would walk through different locations such as shopping areas, beaches, and parks with other dogs. The sole purpose of the class was the honing of each dog's social skills.

Pepper continued to evolve in all aspects of her life and even became a great advertisement for my training business. Our vet, amazed at her emotional growth, began to refer clients to me. Neighbors who had once witnessed Pepper pulling on walks, lunging at passersby, and exploding when she saw trucks, now saw a calm dog. Referrals flowed from them as well. In fact, she became so calm around people that when there were a few burglaries in my neighborhood, rather than risk leaving her home I brought her to work with me, where she became everyone's favorite.

Life was a series of serene days until October 29, 2012, when Long Island was devastated by Superstorm Sandy. Pepper and I spent seven hours in a utility closet riding out the ravages of the storm, which caused well over 100 deaths, damaged 200,000 homes, left 8 million people without power, and caused in excess of $50 billion in damage. For the duration of the storm Pepper, who clearly knew something was amiss, rode it out under my covering body, rarely moving. As I shielded her from possible harm, I understood the instinctive drive that motivates parents to protect their children. I'm convinced our bond grew even stronger because of those seven hours.

As much as my relationship with Pepper had blossomed, it stood in stark contrast to how Jan and I were faring. Despite numerous stops and starts, in the end we were the Sisyphus of relationships, never quite making it to the top of the hill before rolling back to the bottom.

Financially, I hadn't rebounded from the recession. The value of my home plummeted. My savings took a colossal beating, compounded by my nose-diving income. In large part due to the corruption of the owners, who possessed scruples somewhere between that of a roadside fortune teller and a pickpocket, the printing company in which I was employed went bankrupt. The writing was on the wall — my days in New York were numbered. Unless I was willing to work 60 hours per week, I simply couldn't stay. While I had never been afraid of hard work — I was the son of the hardest working man I have ever known — long work hours weren't an option since it meant Pepper would be spending far too much time alone. More importantly, I was aware that even though she hadn't yet shown signs of aging, her senior years were around a distant, yet visible, corner. Being available to help her through them wouldn't be possible while spending the majority of my time at a job. Moving from New York would allow me that freedom, as my work schedule would be lighter in a less financially demanding location than the meat-grinder known as New York.

While working at the soon-to-be-bankrupt printing company, a coworker, Joe, engaged me in conversation about a seemingly wonderful city where his sister lived: Cary, North Carolina. Joe often spoke glowingly about Cary, particularly upon returning from visits there. In fact, over the next months we referenced Cary with such regularity that we joked about being like Steinbeck's Lennie and George, dreaming of the day they'd be living on their own farm. We even referred to each other by their names.

On a snowy day in February, upon arriving at work I was informed that Joe had died of a massive heart attack the previous evening. Joe's passing was a message that was easy to decipher: *tomorrow is promised to no one.* With this lesson in mind and my financial pressures mounting, it was time to visit Cary.

The day after Joe's funeral, I began planning my trip to explore his favorite city by first searching for a dog-friendly hotel there. The stunningly beautiful, $400 -per-night Umstead Hotel and Spa was the hotel that best met our needs, as most dog-friendly hotels might have been such for the dog, but seemed *anything but* for humans — particularly this human. The following weekend, with snacks and bottled water at the ready, Pepper and I headed south for the nine-hour drive to Cary, North Carolina.

Royalty at the Umstead

The Umstead Hotel was even more beautiful than I expected. Approaching the entrance, I couldn't help smiling as a uniformed doorman graciously welcomed us while opening the doors leading to the hotel's luxurious lobby. Just a few years earlier, Pepper was roaming the streets of Long Island on her way to living in a shelter cage for 22 months. On this day, she was living the good life, elegantly trotting into the lobby with her tail held high and an air befitting royalty. Her regal treatment continued when, a few minutes after check-in, two staff members came to our room offering dog treats and bottled water on a silver tray. When I inquired, "What about me?" I was informed that I could help myself to anything in the room's refrigerator (as long as I was willing to secure a bank loan in order to afford its contents).

Pepper gracing the lobby at the luxurious Umstead.

Pepper's behavior during our stay at the Umstead was nothing short of extraordinary. The dog who had once been referred to as a "graceful brat" by her shelter friend, Louise, showed only her graceful side as she comported herself with a dignity that was fitting for her surroundings. Pepper was courteous to everyone she met, even when being joined by strangers in the elevator. Knocks on our door signaled room service, a highlight for Pepper since I always ordered meals for both of us, and as such were invariably met with sparkling eyes and a wagging tail. Was this the same dog whose greetings of our mailman, or anyone else at our front door, would have intimidated a velociraptor? It was hard to fathom. Perhaps she was making a case for us taking up permanent residence in the Umstead.

Over the next few days, I learned a lot about Cary. It was as lovely as Joe had described and, despite my melancholy over the prospects of leaving New York, Pepper and I genuinely enjoyed our stay.

The morning after returning to New York, while I was preparing to leave for work, Pepper lay down in her bed, trembling. Since we had shared every minute of five full days together, in anticipation of being left alone she was experiencing distress. I bailed on going into the office so that we could practice our old separation anxiety protocols. By the next morning, she was fine.

She often showed signs of a fragile construction.
I'd regularly walk into a room and find her like this.

Despite the time and effort Pepper and I had invested into helping her overcome many fears, the old behavioral tracks that were established long before I knew her remained in place. While we had successfully established new emotional pathways for her to travel, the possibility always existed that a context or event might cause her to jump back to an old track. Such was the case that day. For all her growth, beneath her newly acquired calm appearance she was still a fragile soul and would remain so for the rest of her life.

Selling a Home

In May of that year, I listed our New York home with a realtor — a remarkably miserable experience. In a reversal of roles, Pepper acclimated to each prospective buyer who entered our home much more quickly than I did. Once at ease, she would often follow guests around the house while carrying and squeaking her favorite toy. Seeing this warmed my heart, and yet, her innocence and unawareness that we were going to be leaving our home made me feel like I was betraying my best friend. It was a betrayal framed in a deep sense of inadequacy because due to monetary hardships, I was incapable of keeping her in her home. I had hit rock bottom, not only with my finances but with my self-esteem.

On occasions when I was unable to summon the emotional strength to endure strangers walking through and inspecting our home like a shopper picking out a cantaloupe in a produce bin, Pepper and I would leave for a walk, or a ride in the car, only returning when the house was devoid of intruders. During the walks I'd often feel terribly guilty watching her enjoy all her favorite sniff locations along our usual path. It hardly mattered that relocating was for Pepper's benefit. I couldn't detach from the fact that she was about to be uprooted from all that was familiar to her. After so many difficult, tumultuous years, she was finally enjoying her life and a sense of security. Obviously, I couldn't explain the situation to her, but still I couldn't overcome feeling terribly dishonest.

In July, I reluctantly accepted an offer for our home. I would have preferred to decline it, as I did years earlier when someone made an offer to adopt Buddi, but clearly, that wasn't an option. And so, I closed the deal and the book on my life in New York.

Buying a House

For several weeks, with the assistance of a North Carolina realtor, I had been reviewing listings of homes in Cary. Seemingly, the instant my New York home was sold, all the desirable homes in Cary vanished. Finally, with only two and a half weeks remaining before I had to turn my house keys over to my New York buyer, I found a home in Cary. I wasn't thrilled with it. I was settling because we had run out of time. But given the other option of renting a home in Cary while looking for a more appealing one, and then having to uproot Pepper yet again, this one would have to do.

My lukewarm feelings about the new home added to the mounting stress I was feeling about the move, particularly the prospect of being *totally* alone in Cary. While I had survived, and even thrived through the years of a somewhat solitary existence in New York, being entirely alone in Cary promised to be a vastly different, and very stressful, experience. In New York, alone as I was, I found security in the familiarity of my surroundings, and the few people I could lean on if needed. Conversely, I knew that if there was a problem in Cary, Pepper and I would resemble the proverbial tree falling in the forest with no one to hear us call out for help.

Compounding my stress was my bafflement over how I would manage Pepper and the furniture movers, in both New York and North Carolina. Fortunately, my sister offered to help by supervising the New York location. But in Cary, I was going to be a solo act. Between managing Pepper and overseeing the movers, I pictured myself like the performer at a circus who, while frantically running back and forth, keeps multiple plates spinning on poles.

Given the stories I had heard about furniture movers, I took the task of hiring the right one very seriously. After several interviews, I felt fairly confident that the company I chose wouldn't hijack my furniture and hold it for ransom in an undisclosed location. Subsequent to making my choice, in the hopes of building relationships with the staff, I paid a few visits to their facility. Heck, if my stuff was going to end up in another country, at minimum I wanted to be sure it would be in the hands of people I knew. Fortunately, it seemed like everyone there was a dog owner, so engaging the staff in conversation was easy. I made sure word got out that I was a trainer, mostly by mentioning it every 30 seconds or so while wearing my Rising Star Dog Training shirt. Within no time, I was friendly with darn near everyone in the building — my inner salesperson was working overtime.

With the moving company selected and properly socialized, one remaining priority existed — Pepper and I needed to celebrate the close to this extraordinary chapter in our lives. We had earned a fabulous send-off. A going-away party was in order.

Kathleen

As only Pepper's favorite people were invited, the guest list for the going-away party was short. Most of her Great Tails friends attended, including one of her favorites, Kathleen. During those dark times at the shelter, Kathleen, a long-time volunteer, would often brighten Pepper's life by taking her home for short visits. I hadn't met Kathleen, but through discussions with others, I knew of her and her dedication to Pepper. Aware their time spent together would come to an end, Kathleen was heartbroken yet happy when she learned of my plans to adopt Pepper. I very much wanted Kathleen to meet me so that she could see Pepper would be living in a good home. But Kathleen avoided doing so, mostly because she didn't want to relive the heartbreak. More than four years later, Pepper's party would finally present me with the chance to meet Kathleen and, more importantly, give Pepper the chance to reunite with a loved and loving friend.

As our partygoers arrived, Pepper's affectionate greetings spoke of warm recollections. Despite her happiness, she remained her usual understated and somewhat emotionally controlled self, that is until Kathleen walked through the door. I hadn't seen Pepper's pogo-stick greeting since our shelter days, but when she spotted Kathleen, it was on full display. When she wasn't pogoing up and down, Pepper circled Kathleen and expressed her elation through barking. Kathleen, who had been concerned that Pepper might not remember her, sparkled with a joyful bliss that mirrored Pepper's.

There are times when the emotional impact of a moment doesn't make itself known until well after the event has occurred. This wasn't such a moment. I immediately knew that an indelible picture had been etched into my heart. I'm glad I didn't take any photographs, as they would have paled in comparison to the richness of the moment.

Later that evening, after all our guests had departed, I found someone's camera on the kitchen table. Sigmund Freud believed that people often leave things behind because of a subconscious desire to return to that location. Given the love shared between Kathleen and Pepper, this might have been one of the things that Freud got right — the camera belonged to Kathleen.

The following morning Pepper and I took a ride to Kathleen's home. As we pulled into the driveway, an upbeat Kathleen exited the front door to receive us. Oddly, an equally jubilant Pepper didn't run to greet her but instead raced toward the closed garage. Smiling, Kathleen commented, "I can't believe she remembered." She went on to explain that her husband was not fond of Pepper. As a result, whenever she arrived for one of her visits, in order to avoid contact with him, Pepper's entry into the back yard was through the garage. Over five years later, she still remembered the routine.

Watching Pepper running in Kathleen's oversized yard, purely for the joy of it, reminded me that allowing dogs to be themselves is vitally important to their physical and emotional well-being. And, it's great for ours as well. Simply by observing her race around, Kathleen and I enjoyed ourselves as much as Pepper that day.

Since Kathleen's husband wasn't home, at the end of our stay Pepper and I exited the yard through the house. In the living room, there on a lamp table, was a framed picture of Pepper. In that moment, I felt as if I was visiting a historical site — a testament to a love story. I was reminded that Pepper had her own distinct history, apart from me. About the relationship between parent and child, Kahlil Gibran noted, "Your children are not your children…though they are with you…they belong not to you." Kathleen' s framed photograph reminded me that I didn't *own* Pepper. She was an individual, molded by broad-ranging experiences before our paths crossed. In many ways, as close as we were, she was unknown to me and always would be.

After saying our goodbyes to Kathleen, Pepper and I headed for our final farewell visit, a meeting with Pepper's old friend Matt at Blydenburgh County Park in Hauppauge, New York.

"She's Your Dog Today"

Blydenburgh Park is a richly forested, 627-acre location, which sits alongside the Nissequogue River in Long Island's Suffolk County. Visitors to the park enjoy activities like hiking, picnicking, camping, freshwater fishing, and row boating.

On this sunny September morning, Pepper and I met a smiling Matt in the parking lot. While in Matt's presence, Pepper always projected a subdued and calm warmth, and this day was no exception. She greeted him as if they had never separated, and he reciprocated in kind. As the three of us walked toward a hiking trail, out of respect for their relationship, and in recognition of the fact that Pepper was one of Matt's dogs at the shelter before she was mine, I did something I hadn't before done with anyone else — I handed Pepper's leash to Matt and commented, "Here ya go, she's your dog today."

Matt knew how protective I was of Pepper and how she could be a handful during walks, especially when encountering other dogs. He later commented that when I handed her leash to him, he would have been less surprised if I had handed him a million dollars.

For the next one and a half hours, we enjoyed a leisurely hike. In large part due to Matt's graceful handling of her, Pepper was incredibly well-behaved, even when she encountered other dogs on the trail.

I don't recall much about how that day ended. I don't recall saying goodbye. I don't recall driving home. And fortunately, I don't recall how I felt. As with everything I experienced during those last days in New York, the hours we spent with friends, particularly Kathleen and Matt, were often bittersweet, and in some cases the sadness was so dark that it is still unknown to me.

New York and Sigmund Freud in the Rearview Mirror

The morning after our farewells with Kathleen and Matt, a large shadow cast on my front lawn announced the arrival of a 72-foot moving trailer. The moment of reckoning had arrived. I felt as if I was about to be walked to the electric chair. On the positive side — if there was such a thing — because of conversations we shared at the mover's facility, I had befriended four of the five guys who exited the truck. At least the crew escorting me to my execution wouldn't consist of total strangers.

Armed with a handful of freeze-dried green tripe, a Pepper favorite, I led her outside for our usual greeting protocol. I presented each of the guys with treats. On leash, Pepper approached — and bit the supervisor in the leg. She had singled out the group's *supervisor* for her less-than-cordial greeting. I considered offering to pay the ransom money right then and there. After pulling her back, embarrassed, horrified, and praying for the best, I expressed my apologies and anxiously awaited a response.

With blood dripping down his leg from a single, small puncture wound, her victim unbelievably smiled, shrugged his shoulders and said, "It's OK. I have three at home." Our guardian angels were once again smiling upon us.

Given my experience as a trainer, I should have been more aware. Instead, I had not paid attention to the triggers that, added one on top of each other, lowered Pepper's bite threshold. Trainers refer to this progression as *trigger stacking*. Each time a dog is exposed to a trigger that causes stress, the brain is bathed in stress (fight or flight) hormones. As triggers are stacked and stress builds to an unmanageable level, the chances of the dog reacting with aggression are magnified. The dog's experience is similar to that of a person having a bad day, with a series of things going wrong, until the last mishap, slight as it might be, causes an explosion of anger. Pepper, a very sensitive dog, had been living with her stressed-out dad for weeks (trigger). Navigation in our house had changed dramatically, as boxes in hallways and the middle of rooms upset her normal routines (trigger). A 72-foot trailer had just pulled up in front of our home — for a dog who was phobic about trucks, seeing a truck that size was the equivalent of encountering King Kong (trigger). Five strange men (trigger), wearing uniforms (trigger), were standing on our lawn (trigger). In total, these stacked triggers were more than Pepper could handle.

I had always been extremely sensitive to Pepper's needs, but in this case, due to my own distress, I missed the signs. It would never happen again. To this day, I'm saddened by how emotionally strained she must have been during those tumultuous and stressful days, and I'm also indebted to the supervisor for his response to her bite.

A few minutes after my sister arrived, with anxiety and melancholy simultaneously vying for my attention as homesickness set in, I numbly entered the car with Pepper and began the journey to our new life. Similar to a funeral procession driving past the home of the deceased, we took the last tour of our neighborhood. As we departed the community where we had created so many wonderful memories, I realized I had left Pepper's food and water bowls at the house.

Sigmund Freud knew why.

Not Exactly the Welcome Wagon

After a surprisingly restful first night's sleep in our Cary home (emotional exhaustion has its upsides), Pepper and I ventured out to our new yard for a game of fetch. With so many distractions in the novel surroundings, a fetch ball stood little chance of holding her attention. Rather than simply accepting this, after tossing the ball, I prompted, "Pepper, get your ball." She stood a few feet away from me with an expression of disinterest. With a bit more urgency, to no avail I repeated, "Pepper, get the ball." She then wandered off to explore the garden. A third attempt also fell on deaf ears, except for someone who, in a raspy New York–accented voice called out, "Why don't you get your own damn ball?"

Cary is a city in which very few native North Carolinians reside. For the rest of the state, the running joke about Cary is that the city's name is an acronym for "Containment Area for Relocated Yankees." While prompting Pepper to get her ball that morning, my Bronx-born neighbor had offered his advice from the seclusion of his yard. He was an elderly gentleman who had *New York* written all over him. His name was Helmut, but everyone called him John. Over the next few years, he and his wife, Eva, would provide many warm moments for both Pepper and me. That first morning, after retrieving my *own damn ball*, I enjoyed a friendly conversation with John, which made me feel a bit less homesick. His gruff manner of speaking was always framed with a gentle twinkle in his eyes. Our first interaction did my heart good.

Later that day, Pepper and I departed the house for our maiden walk through the neighborhood. As we did, a Pug came charging toward us from a neighboring home. At first, I found it comical because, after all, he was a Pug and didn't exactly look intimidating. In an effort to redirect him, I tossed a handful of treats in his path, but he charged right past them and began to bite at Pepper's lower legs. Dogs have rules of engagement, and when a dog bites the legs of another, it's clearly a foul and a show of bad intentions.

Muhammad Ali often proclaimed his fighting style was to "float like a butterfly, sting like a bee." Pepper's style, which I had witnessed on a few occasions while saving her from opponents at the shelter and during one walk in New York, was to "float like a butterfly, sting like a butterfly…and run for the hills." All her bluster around other dogs was nothing more than a fear-driven defense mechanism, aka "the best defense is a good offense." At her essence, she was an insecure and gentle soul. This was never more apparent than when involved in an altercation with another dog. Her self-defense arsenal was downright pitiful and on full display as she ran in circles trying to elude the crazed Pug. With each lap, her leash wrapped around my legs, tightening until I was knocked off balance and crashed to the pavement. At that moment, as the Pug was pulled away, I heard a woman with a lovely, lilting southern accent ask me if I was OK. Looking up from the street with my elbow throbbing, trying to be civil, I nodded, and as I did she continued, "Well, I guess *your* dog doesn't like other dogs."

Having traded harsh New York for the more genteel south, and being new to the neighborhood, I recognized the importance of a measured response and a good first impression. While still lying in the street, I blurted out, "Are you f——ing kidding me??!!" I certainly made a notable first impression. How good? That's up for debate.

I later learned that in Cary, dogs are permitted off leash on their owner's property, even if that property isn't fenced. Pure insanity. In all my years with Pepper, there wasn't a single occasion when she was off leash, unless in an enclosed area. Dogs are animals with drives and biological needs. Regardless of how well someone *thinks* their dog is trained — and trust me, most of them aren't — likely there is something in the environment that will cause that dog to give chase. It could be a squirrel, rabbit, a kid on a skateboard, a car, or maybe a guy walking his dog on his first day in Cary. The bottom line? It's ill-advised to think we can override the genetic make-up of a dog in such a way that we're 100% sure he, and those passing by, will be safe while he's unleashed on an unfenced property.

Over the next months, Pepper and I dodged more than a few dogs during our walks. Determined not to alter our lifestyle, I began to carry mace (in North Carolina, this is legal if it's 5 ounces or less) and, in order to fend off any approaching dogs, a heavy-duty, telescoping metal rod.

Finally, I gave up and went in search of an area where we could walk in peace. We found a great path away from any residences, near a greenway only a few miles from our home. For the next four years, twice each day we'd drive to the location for walks on the Pepperbahn.

Déjà Vu

In Cary, Pepper found much of her new world distressing. Most dogs prefer familiarity. Many of her old behaviors and fears we had worked so hard to alter — separation anxiety, aggression toward strangers, severe thunder phobia, and more — reappeared in full force. We weren't exactly back to square one, but we definitely had our work cut out for us.

Since dogs thrive in a secure, predictable environment, the first order of business was the creation of a context within which Pepper felt safe. Establishing structure in her day became a priority. We did so by scheduling all activities — meals, walks, car rides, and play sessions were quite literally planned to the minute. While in New York, we had often engaged in training sessions, but did so loosely, without a fixed schedule. In Cary, we increased the number of daily sessions and practiced at the same times each day.

In the hopes of rebuilding her confidence, I encouraged Pepper to make more decisions. Often, human interactions with dogs focus on controlling them, rather than selectively letting the dog exercise self-determination. Pepper needed to feel a greater sense of self-empowerment. Knowing that she could survive quite well in our new environment, and even control aspects of it, would boost her confidence. As often as possible, I provided choices. Rather than simply giving her a bully stick, I'd offer three different chew items and allow her to choose the one she wanted. She learned that dinging a service bell placed by the door would cue me to take her outside. I loosened many restrictions on walks and even allowed her to occasionally pull on leash and determine the direction of the walk. As often as possible, in as many contexts as possible, I offered her options.

To help her work off nervous energy, I served her meals in work-to-eat toys. While I employed all the standards — Kongs, treat-dispensing balls, brick puzzles, wobblers — plastic Easter eggs trumped all. With half containing food, the other half empty, I'd toss a few dozen eggs in the yard, or in the house on bad weather days. On cue, I'd send Pepper on the hunt. By sniffing through the pinholes of each egg, she was able to sort out the good ones from the ones that didn't contain food. Once found, she would only exert enough pressure to pop the egg open, and consume her prize. Engaging in this game allowed her to satisfy her instinctive drive as a scavenger/hunter and, in turn, reduced her anxiety and stress.

Author's note: I don't recommend Easter egg hunts for all dogs because of the risk associated with ingestion of the egg. Fortunately, Pepper was gentle enough to not do so, but I still supervised her.

All of this helped to set a great foundation, but alone wouldn't have been enough to alter the behaviors that had reemerged, and so we went back to the beginning and repeated the protocols we had used in New York. As is usually the case with resurfaced behaviors, the learning process was much faster than the first go-around. In fact, we were up and running again within a month.

Cary, North Carolina, 2013

Unencumbered by behavioral issues and the meat grinder pressure of New York, we could finally revel in life and each other's company without interference. But underneath the good feelings was a haunting awareness that Pepper's senior years, and all the impacts of them, weren't far off. Much as I tried to push it out of my mind, her slightly greying muzzle reminded me of a similar looking, black-and-tan senior dog we often saw being walked in our New York neighborhood. I couldn't help thinking that given the dog's age, I'd eventually see his owner walking alone. On a cool spring morning, it happened. Pulling up alongside him, I lowered my car window and inquired about his dog. When he confirmed my fears I said, "I'm sorry for your loss. You guys looked like you had a great relationship." He gently smiled, thanked me, and noted, "He was a good dog."

One morning as we walked on the Pepperbahn, an approaching car slowed down to a stop alongside us. The driver's window lowered to reveal a smiling woman behind the wheel. "I work over there at the Allstate office," she gestured. "I have to tell you that I love watching you two every morning as you sing to her, and dance with her. It's so heartwarming to see how much you love that dog."

I thanked her, and added, "She's a good dog."

Getting Goosed

During our walks in Cary, Pepper and I would often encounter geese. Born in Brooklyn and then living on overpopulated Long Island, my previous goose-related knowledge was limited to the non-feathered variety, which Webster's defines as, "to poke between the buttocks with an upward thrust." Subsequent to an event that occurred one day while walking Pepper, I learned that both feathered and non-feathered goose types can be equally unpleasant.

Even with my limited familiarity, I did know that charging after geese just for kicks isn't cool. On more than one occasion, Pepper and I observed this idiotic activity. People, often with dogs, chased after geese purely for the sake of doing so, sending the poor things flying off in a cacophony of honking sounds that rivaled those of any New York City rush-hour traffic jam. I wasn't a big fan of terrorizing geese. I will admit to occasionally indulging in the fantasy of chasing after the goose-chasers, with Pepper, while calling out, "So, how does it feel?!" I suppose I could have been labeled a goose sympathizer, or at minimum, goose-friendly. But my allegiance would be seriously challenged during one spring morning.

All my walks with Pepper concluded with a short run on a grassy hill situated about 50 feet from a very popular restaurant. On this sunny Sunday morning, as we approached that area, we noticed geese by a tree on the side of the hill. No big deal. We weren't going to be chasing them, so off we went for our traditional walk-ending run. As we did, the feathered hooligans took flight, circled, and attacked us. One actually bounced off my head while I was protecting Pepper as she was being accosted by another plumed brute. Being the fearless duo that we were, we ran like hell in the opposite direction. At one point Pepper impeded our retreat by turning back and jumping up toward our attackers, before coming to her senses and running ahead of me. Shockingly, in a continuation of the unjust onslaught, one of the feathered ruffians landed and began *running* after us. It's important to note that when something can fly, but instead chooses to chase after you on foot (webbed or otherwise) a bad outcome is in the offing. It's quite disconcerting to run from a winged, hostile beast in hot pursuit on the ground. On the fly, so to speak, I learned that geese can seemingly extend their necks about 27 feet, so Pepper and I had no idea how to gauge a safe distance. After finally eluding them, while hiding behind a car, with false bravado I shouted, "Hey! Your mother's a pigeon!"

Being that it was a beautiful morning, a crowd of onlookers was waiting outside the restaurant. As they clapped and laughed, Pepper and I headed back to our car. Along the way, perhaps to recover a sense of dignity lost in front of our audience, she pulled slightly toward the geese, as if wanting to engage them. If radio personality Craig Bruce is correct in his assertion that "Nothing surpasses the beauty and elegance of a bad idea," in that moment Pepper was a supremely elegant beauty queen.

Back in our car, driving past the crime scene, I saw the geese had returned to the tree on the hill. One of them was sitting in a straw area at the base of it. I realized she was a mother goose, sitting on her eggs. Her gander mate was standing guard off to the side. It all made sense now. Our assailants would run if chased, unless there was something worth protecting, like family.

During our walks over the next month, I gained a tremendous amount of respect and fondness for the couple. While Pepper was in the car, after each walk I'd stroll back and from a distance toss bird seed and corn. Whenever I got too close, Mr. Goose, who stood watch at all hours warding off anyone who posed a threat, would turn toward me with an expression of "Don't make me kick your butt again" — a warning I heeded without exception. His sense of obligation as protector of his family was inspirational. Through my experiences with Pepper, I was learning that I possessed the same quality.

The gander. "Don't make me kick your butt again"

I was about to learn that I possessed it in spades.

The "Natural"

"She must have had some training before you adopted her," noted Beth, the owner of the Canine Agility Academy. "She just completed the beginner course in only 20 minutes. It takes other dogs several classes to master it." Knowing her beginnings, the chances of Pepper having been agility trained were about the same as her having been taught to pilot a hovercraft.

Fairly soon after moving to Cary, I had befriended Beth who extended a generous offer. As long as I provided advanced notice, Pepper and I were given free run of the grounds at the Academy, even when no one else was present. On this day, after romping about, while sitting next to her in one of the outdoor training rings I commented, "Hey bud, this is why we came here." There were very few times in my life when I felt *at home* — most of them occurred during peaceful moments like these with Pepper.

Proud Pepper on our backyard A-frame.

Seeing us soaking up the sun, Beth approached and offered to teach Pepper some agility basics. Astonishingly, after a few trials, Pepper easily navigated the beginner course, which consisted of an A-frame, platform, tunnels, and a few low jumps. As we were exiting the ring, looking at the teeter (see-saw) I inquired, "How about that one?" I was informed it was for more advanced dogs. Not to be deterred, and curious as to how Pepper would respond, I feigned interest from a trainer's perspective and asked to be shown how dogs are taught to cross it. The demonstration began with Pepper being food lured at the bottom of the ramp. Without hesitation, she continued up that side and down the other, gracefully navigating the teeterboard even when it dropped to the opposite side. She dismounted with a twinkle in her eyes and a "Hey Dad, I did it" expression of pure delight, which I met with my own celebration.

Five years after adopting her, she was still astonishing me with little gems like these. Her unexpected behaviors resembled flowers popping up in our back yard during that first spring in Cary. Having moved into our home in the fall, when spring arrived it brought with it seemingly daily surprises, as brightly colored flowers blossomed in the gardens. In much the same way, a blossoming Pepper provided me with her own brightly colored surprises.

With my interest in agility piqued, Pepper and I began observing the Academy's competitions. During these events, her placid, matter-of-fact demeanor did seem to speak of prior exposure. She projected a sense of belonging, much like she had surprisingly demonstrated during our stay at the Umstead Hotel. As she observed dogs in competition, her blasé attitude communicated, "Yep, not impressed. Been there, done that."

Despite her native talent for agility activities, Pepper's thrills at the Academy were mostly derived from simply walking the grounds, sniffing, and exploring. Her enjoyment was such that it wasn't unusual for her to ignore my cues when it was time to leave. On several occasions, when I opened the car door and beckoned, rather than jumping in she'd instead lie down in the grass. No amount of cajoling yielded any results until I'd succumb: "OK. Let's go for another walk." Then, tail wagging, she'd jump up for another tour of the grounds, only to repeat her amusing insubordination when again it was time to leave. The entire process was replayed until she had her fill and, satiated, she'd finally jump into the car and sleep during the long ride home. At the wheel, glancing toward her with my heart reverberating, I'd place a hand on her and be warmed knowing that she had a great day. It was the perfect antidote for the guilt I felt over uprooting her from New York.

"He's Gonna Kill My Dog"

In April of 2014, some four months after Pepper's debut in the beginner's ring, we accepted an invitation to an Academy event. Upon arrival, we were directed to an area about 200 feet straight ahead, where Pepper and I had spent time in the past. As always, she delighted in exploring the grounds, but oddly, my comfort level was lessening with each passing minute. The facility was much more to my liking when we weren't sharing it, and so I decided to leave. As we were leisurely making our way back to my car, off to the right I heard a woman screaming. Quickly looking in that direction, about 150 feet away, I spotted her and an agitated German Shepherd. At that very moment, off leash, the dog bolted. Barreling toward us, body low to the ground in a feverish charge, this dog meant to do harm. I hurriedly attempted to direct Pepper behind the gates of the small agility ring where, ironically, she had first performed months earlier. But we didn't make it in time. The Shepherd arrived like an exploding wrecking ball. Attempting to block his path to Pepper, I positioned myself directly in front of him. With a maniacal look in his eyes, he bit me in the leg. Then again. And again. The burn of each bite caused me to feel relief rather than pain — he hadn't gotten to Pepper. If only he would keep biting me until his owner arrived. Within the chaotic blur of violent aggression, I half spun, lost my balance and crashed to the ground. While lying on my side, I extended my leg in an attempt to block him. Teeth colliding with my shin confirmed that I had. Holding on to Pepper's leash even tighter, I continued trying to fend off our attacker. Jumping over me, he finally got to her. Lost in the swirl of savage energy, I was confused by the sound of a loud, unidentifiable, primitive wailing. It was Pepper screaming. Our veterinarian later referred to it as the "Someone help me" scream. With his teeth sunken into the back of her neck, he had latched on. His dark and glassy eyes warned that it was only a matter of time until he would begin to thrash, causing her serious harm. Reaching into my right pocket, I retrieved a canister of citronella, and emptied it point blank into his face. I considered extracting the more powerful mace canister from my left pocket, but doing so meant releasing Pepper's leash, and this was no time to allow the fight to get away from me. Her harrowing shrieks continued as the Shepherd held on to her and, frighteningly, began to pull her away from me. "He's gonna kill my dog" kept repeating in my head. Determined to not let him take her from me, and hoping he'd redirect toward me, I punched and then grabbed his face, digging my nails in as hard as I could. Still, he didn't release her. Gripping his left ear, I twisted and held on. This miserable son of a bitch wasn't going anywhere. I screamed for help and, with Pepper's leash in my other hand, I held onto his ear like I was desperately clinging to life while hanging off a ledge. *Where the hell was everyone?* Feeling there were no options left, in that moment, I decided to take hold of his left front leg and break it. Just before I could do so, someone pulled him away.

With separation between the two dogs, I dove over Pepper and covered her body, bracing for another wave of bites that never came. Pitifully, as if attempting to reclaim her pride, Pepper began barking at the Shepherd as he was being led away. Her body was trembling under me as she did so.

For several reasons, it was our last time at the facility.

PTSD and More Guardian Angels

A few days after the attack, I began experiencing nightmares and felt extremely unsafe and vulnerable, even in my own home. Outdoors, a canister of mace always accompanied me, even when walking to my mailbox just 50 or so feet away from my front door. Restless nights were the norm as I dreaded and nervously anticipated Pepper's morning walks, during which I felt utterly helpless. Often, just as I was dozing off, I'd hear a replay of her wailing cries, and startle awake. Other than puppies and small dogs, I declined all training requests. Where I had previously taken extreme interest and experienced great success in helping dogs with aggression issues, I now steadfastly avoided them. Ironically, Pepper rebounded quickly, without any lasting emotional or physical scars. For a week or so after the attack, she'd cut short her yawns and shake-offs, likely due to pain in her neck. But other than that, she was her usual self. In fact, when encountering dogs on walks, she reacted exactly as before the attack. Expecting a reward, she'd look up at me and then continue on her merry way after receiving one. Conversely, with each passing day, my issues grew worse. After a month, I realized if I didn't address them, I was on my way to a full-blown case of PTSD. It was time to get help.

With nothing more than Google to assist me, I researched local therapists specializing in PTSD counseling. From her website, Dr. Heather Thurston looked like a perfect fit. Upon meeting her, I felt an instant connection. While seriously discussing the work required, she'd mix in gentle humor and an energetic warmth that made the task at hand seem a bit less daunting. Additionally, Dr. Thurston believed in action plans and measurable output. Discussion, without action, wasn't going to yield results. This approached suited me well.

After spending a few sessions recounting the attack and its fallout, we proceeded to an action plan. Dr. Thurston recommended a straightforward protocol — develop a list of contexts that caused low levels of stress and then habituate to them. As it was such an important part of Pepper's life, regaining comfort while walking her was at the top of my list. Since merely *discussing* this, let alone doing it, caused uneasiness, the "fix" was not going to be easy. Reducing my stress to a manageable level was key. After much consideration, the plan was set — I'd begin walking Pepper while accompanied by someone. The trick was finding a willing partner. Fortunately, I already had one in Pepper's sitter.

Upon arriving in Cary, hiring a dog sitter was the top priority on my *things to do* list. Living alone, I needed a safety net. If something happened to me, or if my schedule took me away for longer than she could handle, Pepper would need a caretaker. Given my non-negotiable standards for her care, and the fact that Pepper wasn't the easiest dog on the planet, I had my work cut out for me.

After scouting around, I found my way to a dog sitting service and scheduled an interview with one of their staff, Helen Ballew. When Helen arrived, we engaged in conversation and I discovered that aside from being a dog sitter, she was also a veterinary technician who possessed a very good understanding of canine behavior. Helen was calm, personable, and bright, and Pepper took a quick liking to her. While Helen and I chatted in the yard, Pepper approached the three wooden steps that led to the back door. Helen noted, "You might want to purchase non-slip mats for those steps." Little did she know, I had already purchased the mats, and was going to affix them later that day. Her comment ended my search for dog sitters. I loved the fact that she was proactively looking out for Pepper's well-being. Six months later she would be the perfect co-pilot for my PTSD therapy walks with Pepper.

The plan Dr. Thurston and I agreed upon contained a few simple rules. With Helen alongside us, I was tasked to complete one lap around the neighborhood while walking Pepper. Should an off-leash dog approach, I'd hand Pepper's leash to Helen, and then address the approaching dog. Upon arriving home, I would remain outside the house for a few minutes, rather than rushing through the door.

Since Pepper's first walk occurred early each morning, Helen, who worked the overnight shift at a local emergency animal hospital, would arrive at our home in her scrubs to accompany us during our one-lap-around-the-neighborhood assignment.

What a sight we must have been. Looking slightly freaked out, the guy who had dropped an F-bomb on his neighbor during his second day in Cary — who subsequently walked his dog while carrying a heavy metal pole while singing to and occasionally dancing with her — was now being accompanied through the neighborhood by a woman wearing scrubs. Four years have passed since those therapeutic journeys. My neighbors no longer run for their front doors when they see me, but their discomfort is somewhat evident in their half-hearted greeting waves.

During our walks, Helen would occasionally remind me, "You're allowed to breathe." Oddly, I didn't experience fear, but instead felt an uncomfortably heightened state of vigilance as I surveilled every detail of our surroundings. Navigating street corners was particularly troublesome because each one presented a blind spot. But we completed every walk without incident. As instructed by Dr. Thurston, at the end of each walk, much as I wanted to rush through the front door, I remained outside for a few minutes before doing so. My knowledge of operant conditioning, a key component of dog training, provided me with an understanding of why this was necessary. Any behavior that ends discomfort by stopping or removing whatever is causing the discomfort is strengthened and more likely to occur again. In Skinnerian theory, this is known as negative reinforcement. In my case, being outside my home, especially with Pepper, was an aversive stimulus that caused me much discomfort. Rushing into the house would allow me to escape this stimulus, thereby reinforcing the behavior of rushing into the house, making it more likely to occur in the future. Clearly, this was not what I wanted. And so, at the end of each walk, with my heart racing, we'd stand in front of my home conversing about topics that, in the moment, I had no interest in discussing.

One morning after completing our walk, while safely back in my home, I received an inquiry phone call about my training services. The caller, a southern gentleman named Bill, described what he was looking to achieve. The ensuing conversation was fairly typical until he said, "Oh. And one thing I should mention. I'm blind. Is that a problem?"

My training sessions with Bill and Lexi, his year-old Havanese, were as unique as they were rewarding. Bill had a great sense of humor, which he expressed through a melodic, southern drawl. During our first session, while teaching him to cue his dog to sit I complimented, "Well done. She's sitting." With only my words as proof, Bill smiled wryly and responded, "Why should I believe you?" Bill was an easy guy to like.

Toward the end of our session, the phone rang. Bill excused himself. Navigating his way to the kitchen by placing his hand along the wall, he answered and informed the caller that he was busy training Lexi. Returning, he accidentally knocked a framed picture off the wall. Without hesitation, he simply picked it up and rehung it. Feeling comfortable in our give-and-takes I said, "Uh, Bill. I hate to break the news to you, but you hung the picture upside down."

"Not as far as I'm concerned." Yes, Bill was an easy guy to like.

Ernest Hemingway once defined courage as *grace under pressure.* Bill's grace in the face of the daily pressures that challenged him was awe-inspiring. Upon returning home, motivated by his courage and as a reminder that I could confront my PTSD challenges in much the same manner as Bill had addressed his hurdles, I hung one of my office pictures upside down. As it remains to this day.

Our Golden Months

The next 12 months were our *golden* months. Oh, sure, there were a few misadventures, such as having four wisdom teeth extracted and then attempting to get Pepper walked before the arrival of an impending thunderstorm. With gauze stuffed in my mouth, we drove to the Pepperbahn. I figured I could tough out my pain through a very short walk. Mission accomplished, we returned to my car, which was stone-cold dead. Silence can be a wonderful thing, but not when attempting to start one's car. Thirty minutes later, after trekking a few miles through fields and our neighborhood while accompanied by the rumblings of thunder in the distance, we arrived home. Pepper headed straight for her bunker. I headed straight for the Motrin.

But mostly, life was gloriously uneventful. We found great joy simply being in each other's company. No more training. No more behavior modification. Instead, we logged countless hours taking car rides to nowhere, playing all her favorite games, or just watching the world go by. We added backyard senior agility to our days, and even though I was still a bit on edge (and always carrying my dog-repelling tools) we enjoyed our twice-daily walks on the Pepperbahn, often stopping for discussions while sitting under the shade of our favorite tree. Pepper even appreciated occasional houseguests, including our friend Dr. Ian Dunbar. The once-abandoned stray dog was now hobnobbing with some notables.

Pepper and our friend Dr. Ian Dunbar in our Cary home.

My training business was thriving, and my printing sales career, once on life support, experienced a revival of sorts with my new company, TCG Legacy in Garner, North Carolina. My emotions about the printing industry also experienced a renewal, as the atmosphere at TCG was nothing like the noxious climate engendered by the owners of the last few companies I had worked for in New York. And to top it off, TCG was dog-friendly, so Pepper often accompanied me to the office.

A book that I authored, *Fetch More Dollars for Your Dog Training Business*, was published by Dogwise Publishing. A year later I was the recipient of the Dog Writers Association of America Maxwell Award, when *Fetch* was selected as the 2015 Reference Book of the Year. The Award is named after Maxwell Riddle, who was a president of the DWAA and wrote a column for *Dog World* magazine for 50 years. In his day he was known as the greatest authority on dogs. As further confirmation of the book's value, a major pet-supply retail chain contracted a bulk purchase and invited me to speak at their annual conference. This was all pretty heady stuff for my maiden publishing voyage. In true George Costanza pessimistic fashion, I figured, "Well, my life as an author is all downhill from here."

Other than showing some early signs of arthritis in her right hip, confirmed in an X-ray that also revealed she had suffered a broken pelvis at some point in her life, Pepper was in good health. To mitigate any discomfort caused by her arthritis, we began cold laser therapy treatments on her hip, as well as continuing her daily doses of joint-health supplements. Fortunately, her bloodwork had been perfect for years, showing no liver issues linked to the hepatitis she had been diagnosed with while living at the shelter.

In fact, my greatest concern for Pepper's health came in the form of copperhead snakes. I had only learned about them just prior to moving to North Carolina. Living in New York, there were no venomous snakes. Informed of their existence in Cary, I handled the news with quiet dignity and grace — I freaked out like a 9-year-old child locked in a room full of big, hairy, ill-tempered spiders. Over the next several weeks, when meeting people in the neighborhood I introduced myself by saying, "Hi. I'm John. Have you seen any snakes around here?" Although I wouldn't want one on my bowling team, I sort of accept a snake's right to exist. My concern, as always, was Pepper, especially given her very high prey drive. And so, during our time in Cary, she was always accompanied by me while in the back yard. Without any supporting proof, I suspect this somehow led to an interesting new behavioral quirk — Pepper's rules of no backyard pooping. The guidelines, as far as I could tell, were quite simple. The back yard was for urinating only. Bowel movements were saved for the Pepperbahn. There were no such rules when we lived in New York. While I refer to this newly acquired behavior as a *quirk*, truth be told, it would become hugely problematic and the cause of serious issues later.

Pepper 2015

But for now, we basked in the glow of an idyllic life.

Mortality

In March of 2015 our stellar and very caring veterinarian, Dr. Diona Krahn, diagnosed Pepper with a grade I heart murmur. Because Dr. Krahn embraced my need to partner in decisions, and respected my tendency to be overprotective of Pepper, I was permitted to observe the confirming echocardiogram test. "She's the calmest dog we've ever worked with," noted one of the technicians. Pepper had surely come a long way since her days when veterinarians would not examine her if she wasn't wearing a muzzle.

While I was proud of her, and relieved to be with her during the test, seeing the malfunctions of Pepper's heart in stark, live video capture, was an atrocious experience. Heart murmurs, which typically impact smaller dogs more frequently than those of Pepper's size, often present a serious risk for congestive heart failure when fluid volumes within the deteriorating heart increase. Based on Dr. Krahn's advice, which I always trusted, we started Pepper on enalapril. The drug helps regulate blood pressure by easing the stress on blood vessels, thereby increasing the supply of blood and oxygen to the heart, helping the heart to operate more efficiently. Since the potential for side effects was minimal, the decision was an easy one. Even though she was asymptomatic, I began to chart Pepper's resting heart rate on a twice-daily basis. Increases in a dog's resting heart rate are often indicative of a worsening murmur. Fortunately, Pepper's heart rate never exceeded 60 beats per minute — a very good thing. And not that I knew what I was listening for, but I also purchased a stethoscope and regularly listened to her heart. Dr. Visconti was in the house. I finally had an excuse for my bad penmanship.

Even though Pepper's murmur wasn't life-threatening, I was confronted with tangible evidence of her mortality. I had been experiencing low levels of anticipatory grief almost from the day I brought her home. In fact, in hindsight, my somewhat slow path to adopting her was in large part related to my fear of losing her. The uncovering of the murmur greatly turned up the volume of my fears, motivating me to seek guidance.

A few weeks after the diagnosis, I scheduled an appointment with a clinical counselor at the NC State College of Veterinary Medicine, Dr. Jeannine Moga, who specialized in grief counseling. During our first session, and future ones over the next few years, Dr. Moga, with a gentle demeanor and understanding smile, provided perspectives of great value. But the most powerful takeaway from our discussions was simply my sense of being understood — Dr. Moga recognized the unique nature of the relationship Pepper and I shared.

Even if just for a few hours, Dr. Moga's office was "home."

Clues

"I don't know how to describe it. It looks as if she is continually resetting her right paw," I explained to Dr. Krahn, vainly hoping she could picture what I was seeing: Pepper lifting her paw slightly, numerous times in quick succession. I also mentioned that in the past week, on two occasions Pepper had shown discomfort in the same leg while rising after sleeping. After a full exam, Dr. Krahn offered some possible causes for the symptoms, and strongly recommended that I bring Pepper to NC State College of Veterinary Medicine, consistently ranked as one of the best in the country, for an extensive neurological examination. One month later, in August 2015, Pepper was put through the paces during a session that lasted for over an hour. She was remarkably well-behaved and tolerant while being poked, prodded, and manipulated by several people. Truth be told, the university found her a much easier patient to work with than me, as I was by her side supervising and asking questions during the entire examination.

A few days after the exam, I received Pepper's assessment report, which noted moderate caudal lumbar (lower back where the tail meets the body) pain and mild cervical (neck) pain. A decreased range of motion in her problematic front right leg was also noted. Likely due to "favoring" it to avoid arthritic discomfort, measurements of her back-right leg showed muscle mass that was less than her left leg, Treatment recommendations included heat, stretching, and walks. Gabapentin, a drug often administered in concert with other drugs as a treatment for chronic pain in dogs, was prescribed.

Over the next few months, with some adjustments, Pepper and I maintained our usual routines. Considering her cervical spine issues, to reduce the chances of worsening the condition I began lifting her out of the car, rather than allowing her to impact the ground. I also cobbled together a set of portable steps out of styrofoam topped with nonslip pads for her to use when entering the car. Even though the bar was at the lowest setting, I removed the high-jump apparatus from our backyard agility course. Her twice-weekly cold laser treatments were extended to also include the problem area in her neck. Every morning and evening, I applied heat to the affected areas of her body and gently manipulated her limbs with some light stretching and massage.

While I wasn't blind to what was happening, with my new plans in place I felt that I had the situation under control. But I was about to learn a lesson. In the words of author Allen Saunders, "Life is what happens to us while we're making other plans."

Life-Changing Fall

At 9:30 p.m. on January 24, 2016, the evening's calm was shattered by ear-piercing screams. Racing into the living room, I found Pepper on the couch lying on her side, head down, with her mouth frozen open in a horrific expression of agony. As I reached to comfort her, she snapped at me and again began wailing. If she had wanted to, she could have bitten me, but even in the throes of excruciating pain, she chose not to. Heeding her warning, I stopped trying to help and sat on the floor next to her. Within a few seconds, she quieted and simply arose, and as if nothing had happened, she jumped down from the couch and made her way into the den. Fearing the worst, rather than allowing her to lie down on the floor, which would again put her in a position where I couldn't help, I directed her to the nearest bed. From there, I could more easily lift her if necessary. Within a few seconds, the horror repeated itself. She again began to shriek.

Taking hold of the side of her bed, I gently lifted until she was standing. I then carried her to the car and carefully placed her on the seat. A few minutes later, we arrived at a local emergency clinic, NCE Animal Hospital. In order to get the lay of the land, I hurriedly made my way into the building to check out the lobby and then raced back to the car. From there, I carried Pepper through the front doors. Rather than risking her losing her balance on the tile floor, I stood with her in my arms while explaining our situation to a technician. We were immediately led to an examining room where, within a few minutes, Dr. Emily Alexander appeared. I once again recounted what had happened. Dr. Alexander listened attentively and sympathetically. She asked if any event or accident had occurred that might have triggered the episode.

And it struck me. The previous day, Cary was hit with an ice storm. That morning, because of Pepper's iron-clad rule about refusing to use our back yard for anything but urinating, and because the yard was patched with ice, we drove to the Pepperbahn. I carried her from the car to a nearly ice-free area where I watched as she unsteadily walked on a stretch of grass. As I tried to steer her away from an ice patch, she instead chose to go in the opposite direction, slipped on the ice, and fell off the curb into the street.

Dr. Alexander asked a few follow-up questions before taking Pepper to another area of the hospital. It was the first time since I had adopted her that I wasn't with Pepper during an exam. Fifteen or so minutes later Dr. Alexander and a very groggy, unsteady Pepper returned. To ease her pain, an injection of Demerol had been administered. As I sat on the floor with Pepper in my arms, Dr. Alexander provided a full explanation about the likelihood that Pepper's ailment was cervical intervertebral disc disease (IVDD).

IVDD is a condition where the cushioning discs between the vertebrae bulge or rupture into the spinal cord, causing the discs to press on the nerves. The pressure can cause extreme pain, nerve damage, and even paralysis.

I later learned that Pepper's condition was chronic. With chronic IVDD, the symptoms can be very subtle, if apparent at all. Pepper's IVDD likely dated back to before I noticed her resetting her front paw and exhibiting tremors in the same leg. Both symptoms were caused by compression of the nerves in her spine. In hindsight, beyond the paw resetting and spasms, I realized I had seen the subtlest symptoms during the previous months. Her fall on the ice was an acute event that, when coupled with the underlying chronic condition, led to the extreme pain she had experienced that evening.

Because of the risk of reinjury, Dr. Alexander explained that Pepper's activities would need to be restricted and closely monitored. Climbing up and down stairs was no longer permitted. Jumping off the couch was also deemed to be dangerous. Even car rides could be hazardous. Additionally, anything that could cause her to strongly react, such as the arrival of the mail truck or landscapers at our home, presented a danger. And sadly, walks along the Pepperbahn with its many distractions were now a best-avoided, high-risk activity.

In the early morning hours, we left the hospital with prescriptions for gabapentin, carprofen, tramadol, and methocarbamol, and much trepidation about what the future might hold.

In the proverbial blink of an eye, life as we had known it had ended.

Lockdown

Returning from NCE, the first order of business was to establish an area in the house where I could monitor Pepper while she healed. As she waited in the car, I blocked off the den with furniture, tables, chairs, and anything else at my disposal. I then moved three of her favorite beds into the room. It would be our living quarters for the next month.

The rest of the evening was pure hell. She continually paced without respite and didn't settle until sunrise, a side effect of the Demerol. As morning broke, she needed to go outside for a bathroom break. Because stair-climbing was forbidden, I carried her to the yard, but only after checking to see that my neighbor's dogs — two highly reactive Pekingese who, upon seeing Pepper, always charged toward the fence, causing her to do the same — weren't in their yard. I was now confronted with a new problem. As noted earlier, Pepper had developed an iron-clad rule for using the back yard only for urinating. Now what? I could drive her to the Pepperbahn, where she might put herself in harm's way by reacting to something in the environment. Or, while running the risk of being spotted by the two crazed Pekingese, in the hopes of scoring a bowel movement I could continually carry her to the back yard. I opted for the latter. Some 40 hours passed, and after well over 20 trips to the yard, I was still waiting. Finally, after one last attempt, we took a ride to the Pepperbahn where she "delivered" within 20 seconds. Moving forward, this was clearly going to present a huge problem.

Managing Pepper's reactivity during her recovery was an arduous task, especially because I was doing so without any assistance. One misstep on my part. One overlooked potential problem. One mistake. And her life could be over. The ceaseless need for hypervigilance was the equivalent of balancing explosives on my head 24 hours a day, during a windstorm. One false move and there would be hell to pay.

Since she was no longer permitted to use stairs, I hired a handyman to build a 16-foot ramp leading to the back yard, and a slightly shorter one in the garage. Each ramp's length was covered with non-slip, corrugated rubber surfaces. The one-step thresholds leading to the sunroom and backyard deck were now covered with adjustable ramps. Along 100 feet of the perimeter of the garden, I installed fencing as a barrier to block her access to the highly reactive Pekingese twins. For safe measure, to block the view from either side, I stapled a 4-foot-high, dark green privacy mesh netting tarp to the entire length of the fence. To make the yard smaller and more manageable, I placed garden fencing in the center, effectively reducing it by half. To prevent her often volcanic reactions to front door arrivals, I roped off the steps and hung a sign displaying my phone number and instructions to use it if needed. The door remained closed for the next 18 months. For good measure, I also disconnected the doorbell. Inside the house, all tile and wood surfaces were covered with rugs and non-slip mats, and pressure-mounted gates now separated all rooms.

Following the advice of both Dr. Alexander and Dr. Krahn, car rides were mostly suspended. Whenever I had to leave the house to run an errand, Helen would sit with Pepper while I raced through what needed to be done. On the very rare occasions when Helen wasn't available, because it was less of a risk than leaving her alone in the house, Pepper would accompany me. With her in the car, I drove as if I was transporting a stack of valuable antique dishes on the passenger seat. During one of these rare outings, I was warned about driving too slowly by a police officer who pulled up alongside us. Thankfully, he issued his warning from his car rather than pulling me over. Pepper would not have reacted well to a guy in a uniform approaching our car, and the result would have been disastrous. In response to his admonition, I threw Pepper under the proverbial bus, noting that it was all her fault. After repeating his warning, he smiled and drove off. I might be the only Corvette driver who has been warned for driving too *slowly.*

When it was time to settle down for sleep, eight hours of binaural music, which has been said to aid in healing, serenaded us until the morning. While there's no scientific evidence to support this, and while the droning nature of the music struck me as resembling the soundtrack to an Alfred Hitchcock movie, I was willing to try anything that might have helped Pepper to heal.

One freezing cold morning, our path to the yard was made impassable as the ramp was covered with a thin sheet of ice. I spent the next 10 minutes melting it by pouring buckets of hot water. While much of that first month was crazy-making stressful, I often experienced a sense of adventure and accomplishment when devising ways to solve or avoid problems. Over time, those feelings would devolve into physical and emotional exhaustion and an ugly sense of haunting inevitability.

Redefining Good Fortune

By March, there were no recurrences of the event that sent us to the emergency clinic. Pepper was mostly able to rise from a lying position without any issues, even on the days when it was evident she was in discomfort. Her full body shake-offs had reappeared. She awoke from naps and a full night's sleep with an elongated body stretch and crossing of her back legs, whereas previously the disc issues would cause her to abort at the halfway point. Generally, she was much less restless. Despite all the progress, she was still resetting her right forelimb. Because of this, we again paid a visit to Dr. Krahn. During the exam she asked if I was OK with her manipulating Pepper's neck to assess her healing. She assured me that she'd proceed slowly and gently, and would stop at the first sign of discomfort. Understanding the necessity and trusting her, I took a deep breath, dug my fingernails into the back of my hand, and nodded my approval. As Dr. Krahn gingerly maneuvered Pepper's neck, Pepper showed no signs of pain. Given where we were just a few weeks earlier, this was tremendous progress.

Upon returning home, a very energetic Pepper (perhaps she too liked the results of Dr. Krahn's exam) sprinted down the ramp to the back yard. As she began to run toward the dividing fence in the middle of the lawn, fearing that she'd stop short and hurt herself, I called to her. She kept running. I repeated myself with more urgency. At the last moment, rather than heeding my calls, she instead leaped over the fence. The moment shifted into slow motion as I watched her gracefully sail through the air, and then like a ballerina, softly land. She spun to look at me with a joyful expression that proclaimed, "Can ya believe what I just did!?" and then pranced around the yard with the same elation she showed during her proud and blissful dance at Mira's Olympics. Conflicting emotions washed over me while I watched her celebrate her achievement. I was still upset over the potentially horrible outcome of her leap, and yet I felt blessed to have shared in her jubilant celebration of life.

In the coming months, whenever I was exhausted and feeling forlorn about her health, Pepper would do something like her back yard fence leap to announce there was a vibrant, undampened life force inside her. Perhaps she had acquired this self-uplifting trait as a survival mechanism during those trying first five years of her life. Perhaps it was a native quality that predated those very difficult years. She didn't harbor feelings about the past and never gave license to worrying about the future. She only knew the now. Neither yesterday nor tomorrow was of consequence today. It was a lesson she would teach me time and again. When things looked their worst, she'd rally, and in doing so, inspire me to do the same. She taught me the importance of redefining good fortune, particularly during trying times. Six months prior, I would not have classified either one of us as being fortunate to find ourselves in the position we were in. But as long as I could find something positive in the present, I felt blessed. I didn't contrast her current physical state to years gone by. I contrasted it to yesterday and in some cases, the previous few hours. If improvement was evident, life was good.

A few days after Pepper's physical exam, Dr. Krahn placed a call to a neurologist at NC State for a second opinion. Of particular concern were the recurring issues with Pepper's right forelimb. Prior to the call, Dr. Krahn emailed the neurologist a short video I had recorded of Pepper resetting her paw. After considering the recommendations and options provided by the neurologist, such as increased medication or an MRI to determine if surgery would help, we chose to continue our conservative approach — restricted activity, controlled low-impact exercise, cold laser therapy, daily heat, and massage therapy. While physical and water therapy would have been helpful, the risks associated with Pepper reacting to another dog while at the rehab center outweighed the potential gains.

While managing potentially dangerous contexts was important, an equally serious threat to Pepper's well-being was the loss of core muscle due to decreased physical activity. The weakening of those muscles increased stress on her spine, magnifying the risk of another acute IVDD event. Unless the loss of muscle was decelerated, her overall well-being would be compromised, particularly her mobility and eventually her ability to rise to a standing position. Chronic IVDD isn't a terminal disease, but the side effects can prove devastating. Additionally, the daily unpredictability of her condition was difficult to manage and, at times, emotionally draining, as reflected in an email I sent to Dr. Krahn in early March:

This morning, she awoke with lameness in that right front paw again, so much so that she turned, couldn't support her weight, and slammed full force, face first, into the floor. 20 minutes later, she was OK and walking like nothing had happened.

Overall, she's not sturdy and her condition changes at times, seemingly on an hourly basis. The front right paw, while better, is still the one symptom that is most consistently lingering. When she doesn't reset too much, I know we're going to have a good day.

I feel overwhelmed at times. Hour after hour I sit in the den with her on an unpredictable roller coaster ride, and at times feel like I'm slowly losing my child, family, best friend, and a part of myself.

Same Train, Different Destinations

In June, Pepper underwent surgery for the removal of a skin lesion. I had discovered the oddly shaped, discolored growth on her abdomen while rubbing her belly one morning. Two needle aspirations failed to provide clear results. Other than ignoring it, removal and biopsy was the only option. Due to the location of the mass, during surgery she'd be lying on her back. The risk of damage to her already damaged spine gave me as much concern as the lesion.

In large part due to assurances from Dr. Krahn that she'd keep Pepper safe, I chose to move forward with the biopsy. On the morning of the surgery, I was permitted to walk directly into the operating room with Pepper. Kneeling, I kissed her on each side of her face and told her I loved her before heading back to the lobby, where I camped out for the next several hours. It's odd how, determined by context, the same duration of time can either fly by or take an eternity to pass.

During my seemingly endless wait, I watched animated puppies entering the facility, bursting with energetic curiosity. Smiling staff members soaked up and mirrored their goofy behavior. It all felt terribly inaccessible. I was sitting in an invisible isolation booth — my aging dog was on an operating table. I recalled a time in my life when the last thing I wanted to do was burden myself with the responsibility of owning a dog. And now, bolted to my heart, one had become my life.

By mid-afternoon, Pepper was in recovery. I would have preferred that she remain in the hospital overnight (I had seen what recovery from general anesthesia looked like a few years earlier when I brought her home after a dental cleaning) but felt there were too many risks associated with doing so. Care for her required a knowledge of all her triggers and anticipation of problems that could arise. No one knew her or could predict her behaviors better than me. And so a few hours later, I carried a dazed Pepper into our home.

The next 12 hours were a horribly magnified replay of her recovery from our emergency room visit five months earlier. She spent the first few hours in her bed, whimpering. When she finally arose for a drink of water, her back legs slowly gave way. With my assistance, she eventually made it to the water bowl, but each time I tried to help by supporting her body, she'd stop and stand motionless, refusing to drink. Bringing the water bowl to her while in her bed didn't solve the problem. Eventually, I resorted to using an eye dropper. At one point, lacking the strength to support herself, while sitting, her front paws began to slide forward until she cried in pain when the weight of her body was centered on the damaged area of her spine.

Finally, she settled down in her thunderstorm bunker, a corner alongside the couch in the den. At around 9:30 PM, she attempted to leave the bunker, but couldn't. I coaxed her, to no avail. Chicken proved to be an unsuccessful lure. Regardless of my coaxing, prodding, and begging, for the next 30 minutes she didn't move.

I still feel badly for what I did next. I called Dr. Krahn at her home. Her husband answered the phone. Polite as he was, it made me feel even more as if I had intruded into her personal life. As always, she was caring and empathetic. She advised that if I felt paralysis had set in, since time was of the essence, the best option was to rush Pepper to the NC State Veterinary Hospital. She'd call the hospital in advance to inform them that I was on the way.

The coziness of Pepper's bunker was great for thunderstorms, but it presented a huge problem now, as lifting her out was going to be virtually impossible since access to her was extremely restricted. Rather than running the risk of doing so alone, with Helen living only a few minutes away, I summoned her. As difficult as the situation was, I felt immediate relief when Helen entered the den. Hard as she tried, her numerous attempts to lure Pepper out of the bunker yielded the same results as I had experienced. Pepper hadn't moved in nearly two hours. Taking Pepper's back paw into her hand, Helen noted that it was warm —a good sign. "I think she's OK. I'll lift her bed from behind, you sit in front just in case she needs to be supported." With that, Helen reached behind Pepper and was rewarded with a snarl for her efforts. Undeterred and calm as could be, Helen continued, "OK. I'm lifting the bed now."

Bracing for the worst, I positioned myself directly in front of Pepper. As I did, she stood and began to walk. With my eyes welled, I exhaled and dropped my head to my knees, sitting in an upright fetal position. As I did, Pepper walked right past me — and ate the previously unappetizing chicken off the coffee table.

I once wrote and recorded a song called "Same Train, Different Destinations." The lyrics describe how two very different realities can exist within the same context. With Pepper casually strolling past a very emotional me to feast on chicken, life had imitated art. Clearly, in that moment, we were inhabiting very different worlds within the same universe.

Hobson's Choice

The results were in. Pepper's growth was benign. Great news indeed, but Dr. Krahn wanted to schedule a consultation to discuss her IVDD. During Pepper's surgery, some X-rays were taken of her spine. While X-rays wouldn't be sufficient to diagnose her IVDD, they could provide rule-outs of other issues such as disc infections and bony tumors, and also yield information regarding her arthritis.

During the consultation, Dr. Krahn expressed concerns that Pepper was likely experiencing occasional pain. She also restated her apprehension about our limited ability to mitigate muscle loss due to the restriction of Pepper's physical activities. Dr. Krahn suggested surgery might be a viable option. Disc compression surgery involves creating a small window in the bone around the spinal cord to gain access to the disc material, which is removed, relieving the spinal cord compression and facilitating healing. Since the surgery is effective at relieving pain, physical restrictions could be loosened and activity increased. As a result, the rate of decline in Pepper's overall muscle mass would be decelerated and her life extended. But prior to surgery, an MRI would be necessary.

With a mix of trepidation and hope, I contacted the NC State Veterinary Hospital, the only local facility offering MRI technology. I was informed that a full physical examination of Pepper would be required prior to the MRI. For several reasons, all related to her safety, this didn't sit well with me, but the only other facility offering MRI services was well over two hours away. Given Pepper's condition, the long drive wasn't an option. As a result, if I chose to have an MRI done, Pepper would first be subjected to another physical examination. With the previous somewhat grueling 1 ½-hour examination still fresh in my mind, in the hopes of convincing them otherwise, I communicated the downside risks to the staff at NC State — Pepper could be injured by slipping on the floor, reacting to seeing another dog, being manipulated the wrong way, and who knows what else. I also noted that we already possessed X-rays and a recent examination by Dr. Krahn. My words had no impact. An examination was required.

Several hundred years ago, a man named Thomas Hobson worked as a livery stable owner in Cambridge, England. His horses were employed for several types of delivery services. When the horses weren't working, Hobson rented them to local university students. Since the students tended to choose the more attractive horses, many of them became overworked. To remedy this, Hobson began to rotate the horses in the stables, giving students a choice — take the horse nearest the stable door or none at all. This rule of "free" choice ("take it or leave it") became known as *Hobson's choice.*

Exercising my freedom of "choice," I grudgingly chose to move forward with the required examination.

An Unanswered Prayer

As if things weren't already stressful enough, the evening before the examination brought with it a raucous thunderstorm. Since her post-surgery episode in her bunker, Pepper had stopped seeking shelter there during storms. The only location where she wasn't terribly upset was in the garage, in our car. Since the summer temperature in the garage often exceeded 80 degrees, I had purchased a portable air conditioner and two fans. During storms, they were aimed at Pepper through the open passenger window. Running the car's air conditioner would have been easier but to do so, the garage door needed to be open. Since the purpose of being in the garage was to minimize the sounds of thunder, the door needed to be closed.

By now, we had perfected camping in the car during storms. Standard gear included an iPad, a portable CD player, a cell phone, water, and dog treats. By checking the weather radar on the iPad, I could predict breaks in the storm, a very useful method for timing bathroom breaks for both of us. The CD player was armed with a recording of brown noise. I had learned about various noise colors, each one with its own unique properties. Brown noise boosted lower frequencies, helping to cancel out the rumbling of thunder, so it was the best option. And, of course, treats were always on hand. Because of our Bunker Protocol work in New York, Pepper was willing to accept treats during storms, so our desensitization and counter-conditioning continued while in the car. Trainers, or at least this trainer, have an odd habit of seeing all problematic contexts as training opportunities.

The following morning, after spending several hours in the car the previous evening, an exhausted guy and his equally exhausted dog walked through the doors at the NC State Veterinary Hospital. Helen was kind enough to reschedule her day and met us at the hospital, not only to help keep Pepper out of danger, but with her background as a vet tech, to absorb the neurologist's assessments and ask questions. I could count on one hand, even if that hand was wearing a mitten, the number of people who gave me a sense of comfort in these situations. No doubt, Helen was one. I had been in virtual lockdown for six months and was already beginning to feel fatigued. Helen's assistance was not only wanted, but needed.

Prior to our appointment, I had contacted Dr. Barbara Sherman, the clinical professor of veterinary behavior at the university. I was fortunate to have been befriended by her not long after my arrival in Cary. Dr. Sherman's credentials were, in a word, exemplary — her kindness and warmth even more impressive. Through our chat, I had voiced my concerns about safeguarding Pepper during the examination. Within a few minutes of our arrival, Helen and I were greeted by Dr. Sherman, who inquired as to Pepper's whereabouts. After learning she had been taken to an examining room, Dr. Sherman excused herself to pay Pepper a visit. Once again, a guardian angel had appeared. The previously unwanted dog and I were in the company of an extraordinary and caring human being.

Standing at the crossroads of a critical and difficult decision, praying that I had the wisdom to make the right choice, when the neurologist returned with Pepper I was prepared to discuss the risks and upsides of surgery. In fact, I had committed to writing my questions and concerns prior to the appointment and had the list in hand. The only thing I wasn't prepared to discuss was what happened next.

"She's a very sweet girl and a great patient. She was wonderful with us. Our findings are consistent with those of your veterinarian. We believe there are lesions in her cervical, as well as lumbosacral spine. But it's not a straightforward case because she also has several areas of osteoarthritis, which are compounding her clinical signs. Because there are so many problem areas, surgery is not an option."

It felt like a death sentence. I had worried for a few weeks about an MRI and surgery. I had never considered neither would be an option. Other than upping her meds, I was advised to continue what we had been doing regarding risk management and low-impact exercises.

We were entering a new phase where the goal would be to keep Pepper comfortable and happy until her days would come to a close. I asked if it would be OK to give her an occasional bully stick, a discontinued favorite due to the stress chewing the stick placed on her neck. I hoped to hear "No. Doing so would be a risk." Instead, the neurologist responded with seemingly empathetic resignation: "Yes, that would be OK. Let her enjoy herself."

Of all the words spoken by Pepper's doctors about her heart murmur, hepatitis, IVDD, biopsies, arthritis, and general aging, this seemingly insignificant remark was the one that rocked me the most. It signaled a new phase — our roads were about to slowly diverge. Where once we shared what I thought was a common path on which I had helped Pepper gain emotional and physical wellness, I was now confronted with the cold realization that she was traveling on her own path, which would see her drift farther and farther from me, toward an inalterable, inevitable ending.

Dr. Elizabeth Williams — A Rose on a Thorn

As we were leaving the examining room, the attending doctor recommended an in-home physical therapist for Pepper — Dr. Elizabeth Williams. Over the next year, I learned she was not *just* Dr. Elizabeth Williams, but an acupuncturist, physical therapist, herbalist, massage therapist, Pepper's best friend, life-saver for both of us, and most of all, an uncommonly outstanding human being. I have written several thousand words in this book describing some seemingly indescribable events, and yet find myself at a loss when attempting to explain what Dr. Williams meant to us. During our once-weekly in-home sessions, she literally kept Pepper alive. She also helped me to avoid melting down during some of the darkest hours in my life. As a way of pointing out the good that is often present during bad times, one of my childhood teachers would say, "Have you ever noticed how often thorns have wonderful roses?" For Pepper and me, Dr. Elizabeth Williams was the most wonderful of roses amid a very thorny time in our lives.

During our initial consultation on August 4, 2016, I was so protective of Pepper that on her way home Dr. Williams assumed she'd never see us again. But see us again she did, every week for a year. After her first treatment of Pepper, I emailed:

An amazing day! She slept through the night. This morning, she awoke and RAN down the ramp. And on the way back into the house, RAN up the ramp. And, she did it again later. We went for a walk. 15 minutes. She was a bit shaky. About an hour ago, we went outside and, like the old days, she started running around me in the yard. I did put a stop to it. Straight line, I'm OK with. Darting in and out and all around, not so much.

I am a huge believer in letting people know when they've done something commendable. Great great job. I'm not expecting this every day but paws down, this was the best day in about two months.

Thank you!

But the roller coaster ride that would rule our lives for the next year made itself apparent the following day.

Hi…

Just an FYI and I promise not to give you daily updates… We had a rough morning. I had to spoon feed her the balance of her food. Pretty fragile this morning. Wouldn't sit. Pitched forward on the right front a few times just walking in the yard.

I guess I am going to learn about "one day at a time." That's going to be a tough lesson for me.

A checkerboard can be seen from different perspectives — black squares on a white background or white squares on black. I had a choice. I could have fixated on the bad days, seeing them as a consequence of Pepper's activity from previous days. Instead, I viewed her healthy days as a rally from bad ones. She would bounce back numerous times over the next several months, a trait that Dr. Williams and I found admirable and inspirational. Pepper often led us through some very difficult times.

After our first session with Dr. Williams, I began charting Pepper's health on a daily log. Tracking her physical well-being provided me with guidance, and also allowed me to see patterns that otherwise I might have missed. When consistent patterns emerged, her daily activities were accordingly adjusted. Keeping records also helped me to feel less powerless in a world in which I had increasingly less control. I was beginning to understand that Pepper's well-being was tied to mine.

Early on, Dr. Williams provided me with two quality-of-life scales that, for the rest of Pepper's life, I completed every week. The scales, in addition to my charts, helped me to evaluate Pepper's health in an objective manner.

Dr. Williams also inquired about my goals for Pepper. "She's never going to be rushed back to the emergency clinic again," I proclaimed. In response she noted, "That's a tall order. She can hurt herself again simply with a hard shake-off." My goal wasn't negotiable because it wasn't a goal. It was a promise.

The balance between safeguarding Pepper, and allowing her to enjoy her life, would be a tricky one. But, I have always believed that when the grim reaper comes calling, he should find us alive. And that applied to Pepper as well. Rather than locking her away in a protective bubble — within which she would be defined as *alive* only by scientific measures — among the thorns, we found and even created as many roses as possible.

A Sense of Purpose

Suspecting that items I crafted to enrich Pepper's life could also help others, I began sharing information about them on Facebook.

Since Pepper loved watching the world pass by our dining room window, but could no longer sit comfortably for long periods of time while doing so, I crafted a padded window sill extension that allowed her to rest her head while enjoying the show outside our home.

The padded window sill extension.

To aid her sleeping, I constructed beds out of foam core and vinyl. The foam core provided her with support, comfort, and most importantly, traction when rising. The vinyl, which framed the borders, allowed her to slide her paw over the side, the only position of comfort for her still-problematic right forelimb.

Foam core, hand-shaped into horseshoes and triangles, also proved to be a great material for headrests, which she used whenever lying down.

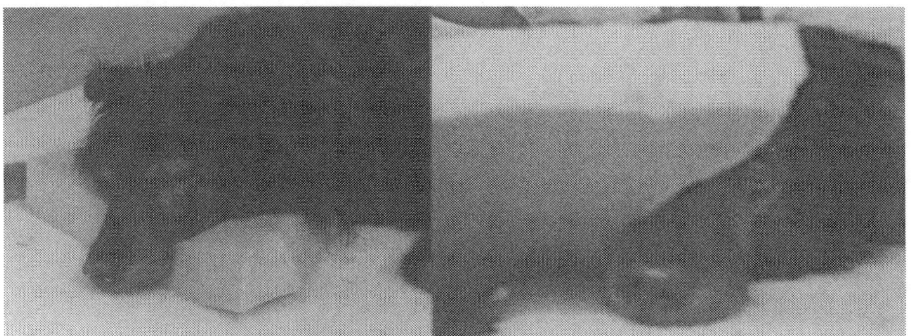

Left: The correct way to use the foam core headrest. Right: Not.

When we reached the point where walks on the Pepperbahn were no longer viable, rather than allowing her to miss out on one of her favorite activities, sniffing, every few days I drove to the Pepperbahn with trowel in hand. Once there, I dug up dirt, pine needles, and leaves near any vertical object that would likely have some dog scents at their base. Returning home, I placed my "catch" in a few plastic bags, punched holes in them, and tied each to the latticework below my backyard deck. *Sniff-In-A-Bag* was a big Pepper favorite, as she'd often stick her head in the bags and revel in their aromas. On a few occasions, I cut low-hanging branches from her favorite bushes along the Pepperbahn and duct taped them to trees in our back yard. Just as with Sniff-In-A-Bag, they provided her with great olfactory pleasure.

Sniff-In-A-Bag

Unfortunately, joy rides in the car were increasingly challenging. While she managed fairly well when rising from a seated position in our home, due to the pitch of the passenger seat, the car was an entirely different story. With each passing week, until I ran out of ideas, I made alterations to the platform I had built over her seat. Options exhausted, I placed a call to a handyman service, saying, “I have a really odd request that I’m pretty sure no one has ever made before.” The office assistant replied, “Oh, we have gotten some really strange ones.” I laughed a bit and continued, “I’ll make you a 25 cent bet, not like this one,” and then went on to explain that I needed the passenger seat removed from my car, and a cushioned platform for my dog built in its place. An hour later the assistant called back quoting a price, adding, “Minus 25 cents.” My newly renovated car was a big hit with both Pepper and my followers on Facebook.

Cruisin' on her new car platform bed.

In a world of increasing challenges, the most problematic one with the greatest downside risk was Pepper's unwillingness to poop in the back yard. In the past, I had twice-daily driven her to the Pepperbahn, but now, with her physical state fluctuating on an almost daily basis, a new plan was necessary. Unfortunately and maddeningly, waiting her out while continually ushering her to the back yard often lasted as long as 40-plus hours without results. Not wanting her to feel extreme discomfort, I'd eventually surrender and drive her to the Pepperbahn, where she'd have a bowel movement within seconds of arrival. After a few weeks of this, I called a meeting with myself and asked, "What would you do if this was a client's dog?" Often a change in context will help in establishing a new behavior. Hoping that a reconfiguration of our back yard would yield positive results, I again called the handyman. The following week, the yard was modified by repositioning a section of fence. After restricting her backyard walks to that new area, the plan, along with food orgy rewards, worked.

In addition to sharing my inventions, I also began posting videos of our exercise regimens on Facebook, along with an explanation of how each one helped us toward our goals — prevention of muscle loss and maintenance of the neurological pathways from Pepper's brain to her back legs. For muscle health, I used sheets of styrofoam taped together into platforms of varying heights, covered with non-slip surfaces. Pepper was cued to stand on the platform with her front paws resulting in her weight being shifted to her back legs, helping to maintain muscle mass in them.

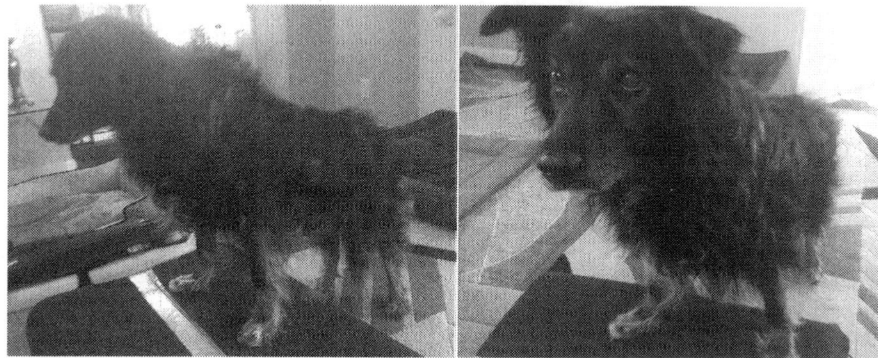

Platform exercises

We also practiced "sit/stand" exercises with the same goal in mind. To prevent sloping of her back due to loss of abdominal muscle (which would increase pressure on her spine), each day, in three sets of ten, I'd tickle her belly while she was standing, causing her to arch her back, exercising her abdominal muscles in the process.

Because Pepper's spinal condition was chronic, continued degeneration could lead to serious issues with her back legs as her brain's ability to communicate with them would be compromised. Dr. Williams prescribed three neurological workouts. She explained that since I had done everything to safeguard Pepper from tripping over items on the ground, it might seem counterintuitive, but placing some low obstacles in Pepper's path as she walked would be helpful. While walks were a great way to promote muscle health, it was equally important to keep the lines of communication open to her back legs. Rather than allowing her to walk on "autopilot," a few times each day I coached her as she walked the yard across a half-dozen PVC pipes

I had placed in the grass. Cones, which she was cued to weave between and around in figure-eight patterns, were also part of the course. In both cases, the exercises required communication between her brain and back legs.

Navigating cones and PVC pipes in our back yard.

Watching her perform her version of "jumping" over the pipes in our yard was a profoundly bittersweet experience. Her expression made it clear that in her mind's eye, as she cleared the pipes, she was the same dog who jumped over hand-held branches at Great Tails so many years ago. Because her gait was now unsteady and her legs weakened, but her spirit still strong, to prevent falls, on numerous occasions I slowed her down as she approached the pipes. But with each hobbled step over them, Pepper's eyes sparkled with a sense of accomplishment.

Additionally, with her neurological health in mind, several times each day I'd prompt her to walk a long length of foam core placed on the floor in our den. Doing so required her to concentrate on her balance, which again was beneficial as it required communication between her brain and extremities.

Along with these videos, I also shared information about our homeopathic remedies, massage therapy, stretching, uses of heat and ice, various supplements, herbs, and cold laser therapy (provided by Dr. Erin O'Leary, a gentle and caring in-home veterinarian recommended by Dr. Williams). I chronicled our use of Assisi loops, which use targeted pulsed electromagnetic therapy to catalyze the body's own healing response to injury, as well as our experiences with traditional medications.

I also shared a method devised to help Pepper navigate the house. While she hadn't shown any signs of cognitive decline, I placed scented oils by her most frequented areas. A small bottle of spearmint was near her water bowl, tangerine by her favorite bed, lavender by the back door. I assumed that should any of her senses decline, her nose would always be a reliable navigator, with the oils providing direction.

One day in early January, weather reports called for snow and ice. Pepper's physical condition prohibited her from balancing or standing on either. In advance of the storm, after spreading the contents of several bags of sand on the lawn, I placed four heavy tarps in the yard starting at the base of the ramp, over which I also spread tarps. For good measure as fallback options, I placed a tarp off to the side of this area, and one by the side of the house. During the evening, every few hours I bundled up, went outside, and shoveled the ice and snow off the tarps. At sunrise, with Helen watching Pepper (she stayed the night to assist us), I shoveled the tarps clean one final time and removed them. I had already repositioned the yard fencing so that Pepper couldn't wander from the clean area onto the icy ground. The plan worked beautifully, as the ground under the tarp was ice-free. But by nightfall, after the surrounding areas melted and flooded the safe zone, it froze over. Fortunately, the ground under the tarp by the side of the house remained ice-free. With a halogen lamp — connected to an outlet in the garage via several long extension cords— lighting our way, Pepper had a safe area.

Ready for the ice storm of 2017.

The Facebook posts and ensuing discussions helped me to maintain some semblance of emotional stability, as I was living in almost total isolation while observing the round-the-clock deterioration of my dog. During her visits, Dr. Williams' more frequent inquiries, "How are you holding up?" were evidence of her concerns for my well-being. But given my charge, and my love for Pepper, I couldn't allow my concentration to drift from her. There would be plenty of time for self-focus in the future — a future I dreaded.

The Ring

As previously mentioned, in February of 2016, just a few weeks after Pepper's IVDD episode and trip to the emergency hospital, my sales training book, *Fetch More Dollars for Your Dog Training Business*, won the Dog Writers Association of America's Maxwell Award for Reference Book of the Year. I chose to not attend the award ceremony because I didn't want to leave Pepper in anyone else's care, but in recognition of my award, I received an interesting gift from a woman, Amanda, with whom Pepper and I had a wonderful relationship just prior to moving to Cary.

I met Amanda at an Ian Dunbar lecture when a group of us joined Ian for dinner. Sitting next to each other, she immediately endeared herself to me when, rather than bothering those sitting nearby with a traditional "Pardon me. Excuse me," she instead departed the table by going *under* it. The gift she sent was a large blue and silver print manufactured by a company that creates graphic representations of sound files, in this case, Amanda speaking words of congratulations for my receiving the Maxwell Award.

That evening, I browsed the company's website and discovered they also forged jewelry from sound files. The following morning, I sound-recorded Pepper engaged in one of her favorite activities — eating from a Kong — and after choosing a black zirconium ring onto which the sound file would be etched, I uploaded it to the company's website. Within a week, I was wearing a beautiful and truly unique ring.

Coinciding almost to the day I received the poor report during Pepper's final exam at NC State, the ring cracked, as if it was reflective of the bad news. I immediately contacted the manufacturer and, with no questions asked, the owner of the company replaced the damaged ring. Upon receiving the new one, rather than switching it with the broken ring, I placed it in the cushion of Pepper's favorite bed and continued to wear the damaged one. Over time, it further deteriorated despite my efforts to keep it together by continually adding pieces of duct tape. And so, I added more and more duct tape until the ring was almost as much duct tape as ring. Superstitiously, I felt its deterioration and my duct-tape repairs mirrored Pepper's decline and my attempts to keep her whole. Replacing the ring would have made me feel as if I had given up on her. Neither one of us was ready for that.

L: The ring held together by duct tape.
R: The new ring (note the etching of the sound file of Pepper at her Kong).

Our Witness

Except for Dr. Williams, no one set foot in our home for all of 2017. The risk of Pepper hurting herself while reacting to a guest was simply too great. But we did enjoy our sessions with Dr. Williams, and I was grateful that Pepper was building a deep relationship with someone other than me. During the sessions, while Dr. Williams physically handled and manipulated her, if Pepper disapproved, she would half-heartedly snarl, but she never directed any hostility toward Dr. Williams. Most often, as if she was melting into the hands of her new friend, Pepper's face softened under a healing touch. Their relationship and mutual trust was a joy to behold.

Months prior to Dr. Williams entering our lives, Dr. Moga concluded one of our discussions by commenting, "You need a witness, someone who can share your experiences." Dr. Williams became that witness. She would often comment on how great Pepper and I were together, or how unique and entertaining she found our relationship. One day with Dr. Williams present, I was attempting to convince Pepper to accept her medications and supplements. She wasn't in the mood to do so. I offered a peanut butter–covered pill. Peanut butter or not, she chose to ignore me. I then circled my index finger on her head clockwise a few times, then counter-clockwise, again offered the pill, and she took it. With a smile, Dr. Williams commented, "What on earth was that?" I mentioned that I had no recollection of how I stumbled upon my discovery but that it always worked. "I don't know what's weirder," she continued, "the fact that she does that, or the fact that you figured it out." At the start of the next session, from my living room, unbeknownst to her, I watched as Dr. Williams offered Pepper a treat, which she wouldn't take. In response, Dr. Williams circled Pepper's head like she had seen me do a week earlier, and offered the treat again. Pepper accepted it. "Remember where you learned that," I jokingly commented, "I expect credit when you use it in your practice."

During a December session, I revealed a new plan I had devised for managing Pepper through the next thunderstorm season. With a gentle smile as her only response I assumed Dr. Williams was saying, "Much as I would like to share your optimism, I don't think you have to worry about next summer."

Uncomfortable with making assumptions about Pepper's life, later that day I emailed Dr. Williams with a blunt question: "Do you think Pepper has six months left?" She responded:

I know it is incredibly troubling to see her like this. Honestly, I think 6 months would be a stretch, but I was also encouraged that again, last week was more good than bad. I think right now, given how much trauma you have endured during this process, it can be hard to see the good for what it is because you know some bad is right around the corner.

We can definitely discuss on Monday, your observations, thoughts, and emotions on the subject. The biggest piece is seeing if her bad days/parts of days are outweighing her good at this point. This is the most objective way to look at it since everything else will be fraught with emotion.

See what tomorrow brings with fresh eyes and chart like you have been doing. I am here for you both no matter what.

You have been an incredible friend and family to her. She is incredibly lucky to have you.

"I Can't Do This Anymore"

During my last seven months with Pepper, I left our home only four times — and not a single time in the final three months. While a declining Pepper had very competent sitters in Helen and Dr. O'Leary, there were far too many risks for me to feel comfortable leaving her with others. Several hazardous events and contexts cropped up every day, each requiring proactive action. Clearly, I was the only one who could keep her safe, as I was the one who knew her best. And if something bad was going to happen, I'd never forgive myself if it occurred in my absence.

By this time, I was doubtless experiencing caregiver burnout. The daily pressures were enormous and unrelenting as I did everything possible to safeguard Pepper. Life had become a series of mini-traumas, with each sign of her deterioration profoundly impacting me. And there was no respite. Concerned that Pepper might hurt herself in my absence, when I showered I was in the stall barely long enough to get wet. Groceries were delivered to the house, and when Helen wasn't available to do so, my very kind next-door neighbor John drove to pick up Pepper's medications.

Worried that if Pepper needed to be rushed to the hospital my car battery would be dead from lack of use (the car hadn't been driven in several weeks) I purchased a charger. And for good measure, I also purchased an air compressor for the tires, one of which had a slow leak.

My sleep was limited to a few hours each night. During the final four months, whenever Pepper dozed off, I'd quietly pick up my pillow and lie down on the floor nearby in case she decided to rise during the night. As a fail-safe, I attached bells to her harness. Should my exhaustion have gotten the better of me, the bells would serve as an alarm system whenever she moved.

If something needed to be done around the house, I'd wait until she was sleeping before addressing it. In one such instance, I dashed out to the back yard to cut a low branch that presented an obstacle during our walks in the yard. Literally two minutes later, when I returned to check on her, I found Pepper on her back, pinned between a table and her bed. She had fallen off the bed. I didn't have someone to whom I could say, "Hey, keep an eye on Pepps, I need to cut that branch in the back yard." Summing up the exhaustion caused by constant worry, lack of support, and inability to control our situation, Dr. O'Leary noted, "It's like you're living in your own personal Vietnam."

On the days her motor skills were compromised by her cervical issues, I fed her by hand. Even though her appetite was still good, she often struggled with wet food, so kibble became the food of choice. Meals could take up to 30 minutes, because during the bad days, I'd feed her one piece of kibble at a time, with each piece at just the right angle, attached to a spoon with a dab of peanut butter.

In June, I began experiencing chest pains. As a result, I emailed my good friend and fellow trainer Matt (different from Great Tails' Matt):

Since I have only slept 3 hours in the last few nights, and only 30 minutes last night, I'm in somewhat of a daze. I've also been having chest pains for several days. I haven't slept more than three hours in a night in several weeks.

Can you do me a favor? I'll e-mail you every morning to let you know I'm alive, if you don't hear from me, please call Helen. I just don't want to have a situation where I'm here and something happens, and nobody knows for three or four days while Pepper is stranded.

While physical exhaustion was a problem, my emotional exhaustion was far more taxing. The only relief from the continual trauma of witnessing Pepper's decline were the moments when, either due to Dr. Williams' seemingly magical therapy or Pepper's determination, she'd rally. But it all had become terribly unpredictable. At times, I felt like the subject of a cruel science experiment. Out loud, I often said, "I can't do this anymore," but would remind myself that I had said the same thing the previous day, and would say it again the next day. Despite how I was unraveling, I was my father's son and surprisingly, every bit as strong.

By this time, Pepper had developed a new habit of snarling, snapping, and even *hissing* at me when voicing disapproval. If she sat up, thinking she wanted to stand I would ready myself behind her to assist. But if she had simply wanted to *sit* rather than rise, she'd inform me with her new method of communication. No harm was meant. It was Pepper's way of expressing herself. I learned to apologize and stop whatever I was doing.

As my emotional reserves approached empty, I found myself in the paradoxical morass of hoping things would end soon and yet hoping they'd go on forever. I took to venting to the few people who were still in my life by coughing up emotional hairballs while speaking with them. While it never felt good to do so, it was the only way to rid myself of the anxiety and stress that were interfering with my ability to care for her. And truth be told, I was terrified about the future.

When her physical condition declined to a point where she needed support while pooping, Pepper's moxie and independent nature led to one last training session. At times, when I reached to support her back end, she'd attempt to spin away from me and, in the process, fall. Or, she would wait until I wasn't looking, and then squat and fall. It was awful for her. It was awful for me. And it was dangerous. Even a slight jarring of her neck could have led to paralysis. Using a harness wasn't an option because she hated wearing one. So, I needed to change her response to me reaching toward her.

For one last time, it was Dr. Ivan Pavlov to the rescue. With treats in hand, I'd leash her up and head out to the back yard. As we walked, I'd stop and reach in the exact same manner as when I was supporting her during bowel movements, and immediately give her a piece of chicken jerky, a new favorite. The plan worked beautifully. Within a very short time, I'd reach, and she'd look up at me with happy anticipation.

While there were still more good days than bad, acknowledged by Dr. Williams who was monitoring Pepper's health each week that she saw her, undeniably the end was near. After dialing the number several times and hanging up, I detached long enough to contact an in-home euthanasia service, Lap of Love, for a phone consultation.

And to order an urn for Pepper's ashes.

The Inevitable

"The inevitable is no less a shock just because it is inevitable." *Jamaica Kincaid*

Prior to leaving for a 10-day conference in Florida, concluding our session Dr. Williams mentioned something about scheduling the next appointment. I responded, "I don't think there is going to be a next appointment." Given that she had never heard me say anything like that before, her eyes welled and she went back to Pepper to again say goodbye. I suspect it was a very different kind of goodbye than the previous ones expressed over the past year.

On July 31 I emailed Dr. Williams while she was in Florida:

Hi... Things are not going well. She's constantly struggling to get up and in some cases, can't. I have no idea what to do for her, which concerns me because I have always known what to do for her. At times I think she needs to go outside, so I take her out and she just stands there. Thinking she might be thirsty, I bring her water bowl to her but she doesn't drink and again struggles to get up. I change her position, and she struggles to get up. It's getting really ugly and I honestly don't know what to do for her. I don't know how to make her comfortable and that also has never happened before. It's possible that today was bad because she didn't sleep well last night. Bad days always follow nights when she doesn't sleep well. But this feels very different. If she's like this tomorrow, well, you know.

Tomorrow arrived. It wasn't any different. Pepper's ability to stand, without my lifting her, rather than just assisting her, vanished. She could walk but didn't have the strength to rise on her own. And she continued to be extremely restless. That evening, she tried to rise for well over two hours. Each time she attempted to do so, I'd lift her up. Finally, to no avail, I tried to calm her by lying next to her.

Over the previous 18 months, I had invested countless hours of thought into the end-of-life decision. Most importantly, I needed someone who knew Pepper and her physical state well, and could provide objective perspectives. That person was Dr. Williams, who had observed and worked with Pepper for 50 consecutive weeks. But, I also needed my own measures. My thoughts included:

- While many people had suggested Pepper would *let me know* when it was time, I wasn't a big fan of mind-reading, especially with regard to taking the sacred life of another being. I knew there would be a subjective element incorporated into my decision-making process, but I was not comfortable allowing that subjectivity to be the primary factor.
- I often read, "Better one week too early than one day too late," but that measure did not apply to our situation. Pepper's chronic IVDD was a disease that led to slow deterioration. Other than the risk of paralysis, which existed from the day she was rushed to NCE 18 months earlier and was something I had safeguarded against every minute, there wasn't any chance for an acute life-threatening event. Additionally, she had often rallied from bad days and deserved the chance to do that, rather than having her life prematurely ended. That said, pain management was a critical factor. Fortunately, Dr. Williams was able to provide a weekly assessment, and I was assessing on an almost hourly basis.
- Rather than adhering to a more standard definition of "quality of life," which evaluates quality by what the dog can *no longer* do, I preferred to look at the list of things that brought happiness that

Pepper *could* do, and what I'd be taking away from her if I chose to end her life. The shorter the list, the more likely it was time.

- If she could no longer be a dog, then it was time. This was my most subjective measure.

- I needed to embrace the fact that regardless of how many objective factors I utilized in making my decision, likely the decision wasn't going to feel "right." If I waited for it to feel right, I'd have waited far too long.

- And I sought the opinions of those I respected, veterinarians, trainers, and others who could provide a perspective different from my own, such as my thoughtful neighbor John, who was kind enough to take the time to explain the biblical perspective about the responsibilities we have to our animals.

The following morning, I contacted Lap of Love. The appointment was scheduled for August 4 at 7:15 PM. Pepper was unaware that she had 36 hours left on this planet. Given that our relationship was based on trust, it felt like a monumental betrayal. Every passing minute brought with it guilt, sadness, calm, panic, and fear. Paralyzing fear.

At around 10 PM, I received a call from Dr. Williams. I informed her that things were looking bleak and that I had set the appointment. With a fragile optimism in her voice she said, "Maybe she'll rally again."

The rally that both of us were desperately hoping for, and given past performance even expecting, never occurred. Her decline was dramatically rapid. Through the evening, Pepper was as restless as she had ever been, repeatedly attempting to stand, until she finally exhausted herself. The next morning she awoke soaked in urine. While lying on her side, I bathed her with a sponge. At around noon, she became extremely restless again. As happened so many times, I instinctively knew the right thing to do. Feeling that she might have preferred some privacy, much as I wanted to be with her every minute that I could, I left the room and watched her from the den. She immediately settled down. Within 15 minutes, she was sleeping peacefully.

Knowing there was a long and painful night ahead, I posted a Facebook thank-you to all who had been following her story. I didn't want to post about Pepper after she died, but rather while she was still alive, as a celebration of her life. I planned to read the responses that evening, in order to help get me through the night and not feel totally isolated.

I have dreaded writing about the next few hours from the moment I created a WORD document called "Pepper Becoming." I am incapable of writing about those hours with anything remotely resembling cogency. Although I can recall every minute in detail, I can only do so as disjointed fragments. Trying to recall them with any cohesion is akin to attempting to pick up a ball of mercury with a hammer. Everything explodes. The mortar required to join those fragments are the emotions I felt during those moments. They're inaccessible. There are no words to describe them. Wordlessness is most appropriate. All else is a mangled translation. But because her story would be incomplete without a recounting of those last hours...

Mid-afternoon...Counting down to 7 PM minute by minute...Reaching out to Jan who provided fleeting moments of comfort...Placing Pepper's foam headrest under her, only to have her knock it halfway across the room...smiling as I looked at her...she was still Pepper...we were still us...all felt normal and calm...a bubble within colorless darkness...Even though spoon fed for days, having a hunch she'd eat a hot dog...She ate it like the old days, without my assistance...Was she rallying again?...Should I cancel the appointment?...Carrying her down the ramp to pee...Placing her down on the lawn...Falling/lying in the grass...Reflexively reaching to pick her up..."NO. It's a beautiful night. This is the right place for her to leave me"...Lying in the grass with my arm around her for the last time...Shelter flashback...Wanting to stay awake to make the time last but wanting to sleep with her...Drifting off with her...Waking up thinking she had taken me to where she'd soon be going...Helen arriving...I hadn't changed my shirt in over a week...Going inside to change and to allow Helen to say goodbye...Veterinarian calling from the road, "I'm 20 minutes away"...Is there a way to escape this? We've always escaped before...Vet's phone call from the driveway...First words, "We all want our dogs to die in their sleep. It rarely happens. We're going to let Pepper die in her sleep."... "Let me know when you're ready"....Stalling...Frightened...OK... "I'm going to give her a sedative injection and when I do, I'm not going to be her best friend"...Asking Helen to hold her in place while the vet administered the injection...I had safeguarded Pepper for so long and didn't want to screw up right at the end...Pepper snapping her head and seeing Helen...Gently rested her head in the grass again...Reaching to place my hand on her head...She bit me, gentle...The warmth of her mouth on my hand...She knows something is wrong... Reaching for her again, and saying "Hey, now was that necessary?" in the soft funny way we always communicated with each other...It all still feels like every day in our lives...What the hell is going on?... Helen saying to the vet, "Oh it's OK. That's just Pepper being Pepper"...Pepper bites me again... Soft again...Yeah, no one would understand...It's OK, Pepps, we're still us...As she was beginning to doze, my face pressed to hers while lying next to her..."Hey Pepps. I'm so proud of you. You should see all the messages you got from people. You touched so many lives. See Pepps, all along. You've been a special dog your entire life"... "Hey bud, thank you. I thought I was staying strong for you, but it turns out that you were staying strong for me until I was able to reach this moment."...Looking up and seeing the tourniquet be applied...Punching the ground...betrayed...powerless...Ripping at the dirt...Helen, "Keep talking to her John"... "I love you bud. I love you bud. I love you bud." Face pressed to hers while she slept...Not knowing when the IV line was put in...She just left...Asking Helen,"Is she gone?"..."Yes"...Turning my back...Removing the duct-taped ring. Placing the new ring on my finger, Raising my head and looking toward the sky...."You got rid of your old broken body and got a new one. I am getting rid of my old broken ring and getting a new one"...Kissing her...Walking away...Feeling the need to go back but not knowing why....Kneeling down and inhaling her scent in the hopes I could imprint it forever...Horrible relief...Emptiness.

Later that evening, our friend Dr. Williams called. With expectation in her voice she asked, "Did she rally?"

"No. She's gone."

One year to the day Pepper met Dr. Williams, she was gone.

A few days later, I received an email from Dr. Williams.

Dear John,

I feel truly blessed that I was able to be a part of yours and Pepper's life for the last year — to witness the human-animal bond at its finest.

We are so lucky to be able to enjoy these animals as they were created. You, especially, have learned to appreciate what a dog truly is and how they truly are our best of friends. No questions, no judgment (well Pepper may have judged a little ;))

I wish I could have seen you and her in your heyday. I bet it was something. I get little glimpses on your website and in the videos you have sent me. I see that relationship and know it was a work of art, love and trust (and a lot of chicken).

You came to her in her time of need and I am willing to bet it was in your time of need as well. This grows the best friendships. It was probably a 'you move, she moves' relationship. I got to see the 'she moves, you move'.

I wish more people could experience the purity of a dog-loving relationship like you did. I wish more dogs got to feel as safe and secure as she did the latter half of her life. Even though she had her Pepperisms, these were born of her nature and some were a result of the first part of her life. You accepted these quirks and instead of pushing her outside her comfort zone, you brought that zone to her. This is special and worth noting. So many times we want them to conform to our lives without regard to their real feelings and worries. They have them.

I so wish I could have been there for her final moments. I will truly miss her and I tear up when I think of her and that I don't get one more good-bye. I have my final image of her burned in my mind and it was good. It's like a snapshot in time. I have been wearing her necklace since she passed. She has been with me on my trip. It's fun when people ask about it because then I get to talk about her!

Some dogs love unconditionally without thinking twice who they are loving, and that is great for some people and some dogs. Some dogs, like we have said, require a little something more, a little extra, and for Pepper, that was definitely respect. She commanded respect and I believe also intelligence. She made us work for it and that made me love her even more. I miss that paw….

I hope you have been OK this past week and are readjusting to your new life. I know it feels weird and a little empty. I am sure this void is huge right now and is hard to imagine how it can be filled. That's the great part about our hearts though, it expands so we don't have to try and fill the void, we just have to make it bigger with new life.

Always remember Pepper's zest for life, her spunk and her attitude, and embody it when needed!!

I will miss you both. Always stay in touch and thank you again for trusting me with your dear one.

Always,
Elizabeth

But Mostly, I Wait

Sitting alone in the house afterward, I struggled a bit with the fact that Pepper's last communication with me was to bite me twice. But as so many times before, she was incredibly gentle about it. She never wanted to hurt me. And Pepper, being the good soul she was, didn't direct a bite at Helen. She looked up, saw Helen and seemingly realized it would be inappropriate to do so. But me? She seemed comfortable enough to say, "Hey Dad. This sucks," in the only way she knew how. As Helen said, "It's OK. It's just Pepper being Pepper," and for Pepper and me, it was just *us being us*. Retrospectively, I'm 99% OK with it. But that 1% of doubt still lingers.

Monday morning, I drove to TCG Legacy. I wanted to thank Jeff, one of the owners, for his patience and support during the months I had been away, with or without leave, depending on who you asked. I explained how I had attached bells to Pepper's harness so that I could hear if she arose during the night. Cupped in my hand so that they wouldn't ring and bring me to tears, I handed them to Jeff and said, "I want you to have these as a thank you from Pepper and me. There's only one condition. If they ever ring, call me."

During my drive home, my car (which hadn't been driven in over three months) died. The transmission was shot and leaking all over the roadway. Since the car had 170,000 miles on it, I had previously set aside $25,000 from the proceeds of the sale of my New York home to replace it. That money was gone. Hardly mattered. The only value in going through a difficult experience is to learn about priorities in life, what to sweat, and what to ignore with a shrug of the shoulders and a woof. My journey with Pepper reinforced this belief in spades. Car just died? No big deal. Go buy another Corvette and adorn it with a *PEPPER09* (the year I adopted her) vanity plate. I was dreading driving the old car because of the memories Pepper and I shared in it, from our ride home from the shelter to our drive to North Carolina to the hundreds of joy rides. I couldn't even imagine removing her platform bed from it. Coincidental that the old car failed? Maybe. Guardian angels? Perhaps. Pepper revisiting? I hoped so. Whatever the case, the death of that car was synchronistically perfect. I was relieved to never drive it again.

An other-worldly occurrence graced my Facebook page a few days after my *PEPPER09* vanity plate arrived in the mail. That day, I received an email notifying me that I had been tagged in a Facebook post by Pepper's friend Anne from Great Tails. During her first few days at the shelter Anne decided that Pepper needed a middle name. She chose *Marie*. "Yes," she thought, "*Pepper Marie* has a nice ring to it." Anne's Facebook post was a picture of a car with a license plate that read "PEPPER M" — Anne had seen it on a car in a parking space adjacent to hers, and snapped a picture of it.

Because I had been terribly inactive for over a year, and sleeping on the floor for several months, within a few days of Pepper's departure I was diagnosed with a full-blown case of incredibly painful right hip bursitis. While Pepper was alive, on numerous occasions I prayed, "Please give me her pain." I guess I should have been more specific about my wishes. Technically, I got what I asked for, but the timing wasn't exactly what I had in mind. For the next four months, after two cortisone shots failed, twice-weekly physical therapy sessions with my therapist, Allie, brought me back to health. During that time frame, each time I winced in pain, I experienced a sense of connection. The pain was a reminder of how my spirited and determined dog and I had toughed things out together. Once healed, crazily, at times I missed the discomfort. The connection was gone.

After informing her of Pepper's passing, I received an email from Dr. Sherman in which she expressed her condolences and a request. In my email, I had sent a video of Pepper learning how to consecutively run through agility tunnels in my back yard. Dr. Sherman loved it, particularly seeing how Pepper and I understood each other, and how Pepper navigated several teachable moments. Dr. Sherman felt that the learning process captured in the video would be of great value for the university's veterinary students and asked for my permission to use it as part of their education. The "screw loose" and "untrainable" dog was now part of the curriculum at the NC State College of Veterinary Medicine, one of the preeminent veterinary schools in the world. I couldn't have been prouder or more emotionally moved.

And finally, I set up a memorial by her favorite dining room window containing her leash, my favorite picture of her, her favorite toys, her foam core headrests placed on her bed, the urn with her ashes and the damaged ring hung around it, as well as various condolence gifts and cards. The memorial is framed by two multi-colored lights that remain lit at all times. Every night before going to bed, I stand by her memorial and channel Pepper before kissing her urn, and Buddi's also, which is off to the side in a glass cabinet. I keep them apart because angels or not, I suspect they still wouldn't get along, even though our journeys together were incredibly similar.

But mostly, I wait. Even though I'm unsure of what I'm waiting for.

Nothing Exists. All Things Are Becoming

He is the light of my life and is the one thing that brings a smile to my face every morning, but I do not believe I can give him the most opportune life at this stage. So, I guess what I am leading up to is the question of, would you like to rescue-adopt him? I have so much admiration for you and the late Pepper, and my mind would be at so much ease knowing that he would have a rock like you. Understandably, I know that the answer may be no, and I will have to find another solution for his life and livelihood.

A few days ago, I was visiting with a training client who sent me the above email. Due to her 6-month-old dog's health issues, she was very concerned about the sacrifices she'd have to make on the road ahead. She had already invested thousands of dollars and was understandably concerned about the future.

Before declining her offer, I said, "Have you ever been in a relationship that ended, and as you were considering dating again, you realized that you were comparing everyone to your ex? In that case, it's not the time to be dating — for you, or anyone you meet. It's time to allow your heart to heal and your brain to clear. It has been ten months since I lost Pepper, but I know I'd be comparing every other dog to her and thinking, 'She's not Pepper.' And so, this isn't the right time for me for me to bring another dog into my life."

Upon returning home, I emailed her a draft copy of this book, hoping she would see that the value of Pepper's story wasn't that it proved I was a "rock," but instead that, whatever the cost, Pepper was worth it. I wanted her to understand she had the same opportunity, not burden, with her dog that I had with Pepper. It was my way of saying, "You'll figure it out." In the end, after reading the draft, she decided to keep her dog. Well done, Pepper.

Later that evening, it occurred to me that what I had said about other dogs coming up short when compared to Pepper spoke volumes about our relationship and my love for her. I suppose there are very few people who would look at a dog with the myriad behavioral issues that accompanied Pepper when she first walked into my home and see anything but problems. I suppose if people thought otherwise, Pepper wouldn't have been dumped by her owners and wouldn't have spent nearly two years in a shelter without finding a home. I have often been counseled, "You should adopt another dog. With all of Pepper's issues, you've had the worst of it. Your next dog will be *so* much easier." It's as if people see a guy they think was in prison being offered a vacation on a tropical island, and declining because the island wouldn't be as enjoyable as the prison. I don't want a tropical island or another dog because I never had a dog — *I shared a journey.*

I suppose, in the end, grief is the price paid for love. Absorbing Pepper's pain by rescuing her from a horrible situation, helping her overcome fears, and then caring for her during those last 18 months brought with it an incredibly loving and profoundly unique bond — and a hefty emotional price tag whose payment became due in the early evening hours of August 4, 2017.

The Tao Te Ching offers, "Those who die without being forgotten will endure forever." My life with Pepper shaped me as a trainer, and because of that, unforgotten, she lives on through the hundreds of people and their dogs I have had, and will have, the good fortune to coach. She lives on through the way she shaped me as a human being by leading me to self-discovery and so powerfully demonstrating the value of living in the moment. Even without meeting us, Pepper's journey touched and continues to color the scores of people with whom it was shared. And for those whom she did meet, she left an indelible impression on their hearts.

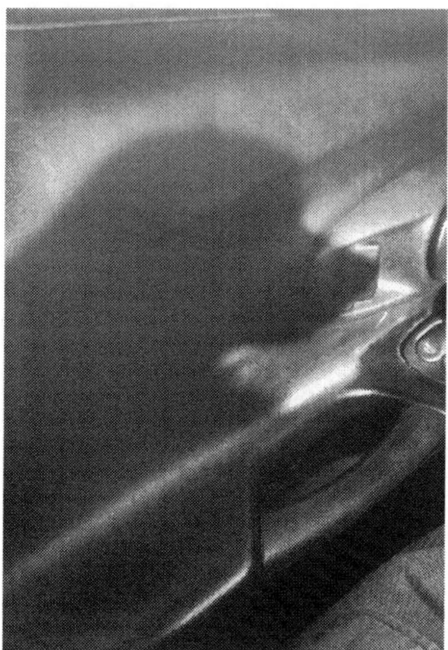

Pepper's shadow in our car.

And perhaps years from now, if this book should find itself between a shadeless lamp and a George Foreman grilling machine at a garage sale, Pepper will live on through the person who spent a buck to read it.

Her transformation, beginning one spring day when I requested, "OK, Pepper. Please give me a sit," through the end of her life, and beyond, has been astonishing. She is the embodiment of the wisdom, "Nothing exists. All things are becoming."

May she continue becoming.

Just a Few of the Lives She Touched

Of the several hundred Facebook responses to my post about Pepper's last day, I have chosen to share the ones that most moved me.

Mira Leibstein: Safe travels to the bridge to my favorite girl. Kiss Targa & Sienna for me. And I hope your papa's heart heals, I know you are his heart dog forever. John, you had longer than you ever thought, but it's never long enough.

Elycia Tenney: Tell Pepper how much she's meant to so many, even those who have never met her! She is a bright light that will continue to shine on, I'm sure of it. Sending you both strength and love.

Judi Hales: My heart aches. She seemed like a very special girl and you were the best daddy she could possibly have. I will miss your posts of her and all of the concoctions you came up with to help her quality of life. It inspires me as my dog ages and is getting some aches and pains, for ways. I can help her to feel her best. She was certainly blessed to be your dog.

Lynn Honeckman: I am so very sorry to read this. You were her sun and moon. Don't forget, "the course of true love never did run smooth." My heart is with you during this time. Pepper was blessed to be loved by you. Thank you for sharing her and a glimpse into the soul of the dog who captured so many hearts.

Ada Simms: You have made her a part of our lives. This is so heart breaking.

Colleen McCarvill, CPDT-KA: While I don't know you personally, you shared her beautiful story and we will share in her goodbye. Godspeed beautiful-girl....

Nil Alptekin O'Boyle: Thank you for sharing your story with all of us. You are a wonderful dad and you and Pepper are so lucky to have shared this journey. Enjoy your day with her. My thoughts and prayers are with you on this difficult day.

Ro Morrison: Together you have borne her trials with courage and such love for each other. Her legacy will live on through the many lessons both big and small that you have shared over the years . You will both be in our thoughts this evening. Run well sweet Pepper - Run well.

Jan Pimm Casey: Thank you for giving her the chance to experience love.

Karen Johnson: I know you must be struggling, but the strength and care you have shown her is so inspiring. Love to you both.

Dennis Anne: Oh my two sweet friends, I am so blessed to have known and loved Ms. Pepper. She is in my heart and so are you John. She was given a life because of you and now her journey will take her over that Rainbow bridge where she will still watch you and love you.

John Esposito: Such gut-wrenching sad news. But I know you saved her and gave her an amazing life John. Godspeed Pepper, you will be missed.

Elaine Marshall Chevalier: I am so sorry. Thank you for sharing your life with Pepper with us. My thoughts and prayers are with you.

Pam Ingalls: So sorry, her story is an inspiration, being in rescue work and thinking no one will want a dog with so many issues but somehow a good hearted person sees past that. It's so hard to say good bye. She was clearly special and so are you.

Venita Bentley: Enjoy your last day together. Thank you for giving her a chance to overcome her terrible beginnings and seeing past the aggression that she used to protect herself.

Denise Armstrong: I have followed your stories about her and truly believe she couldn't have anybody better as her owner. Such consideration for her needs and comfort have been truly humbling to read.

Ann-Marie Brady Levine: Your joys and struggles with Pepper over the years have touched me deeply, in no small part because of your honest and open telling of them. Thank you, John. I'm sorry that Pepper's peace must come at the price of your heartache, part of the honour and privilege of helping to ease them from this life. May your memories see you through.

Joanna MooMom: Sending love… thank you for sharing her story with us. She couldn't have asked for a better human to guide her through life.

Hilary Lane: Thank you for sharing her journey with us, whether difficult or not. You and she were a great team and I am so glad she had you, as she wouldn't have made it through so well without your kind and gentle care.

Valerie Caracciolo Yurick: Farewell Pepper! I loved watching you grow and hearing your story. So sorry John

Eileen Kennedy-Mendez: What a wonderful and storybook love you both shared for each other. My heart breaks for you as you have lost a true warrior and friend. May you know and believe in your heart that Pepper had the absolute best possible life ever because of you.

Suzanne Roche Kolker: My heart is breaking for both of you. She was so loved! I will miss her. You will be in my thoughts and prayers even more often than you are now. I hope you can find the peace you have given her.

Cindy Shauck Murphy: You and Pepper have made a difference in my life and in the life of my "not easy" sweet Bear. Thank you for sharing the highs and lows, even this most difficult of days with us. Know that a tremendous amount of support and energy is indeed being directed to you and Pepper's spirit today.

April Henry: Lil Pepper thanks for being so wonderful and for giving so much joy to your soul mate. I only met you once but I know precious when I see it. Love you so much little girl. Sending you my angels to take you away from the pain and to your next adventure.

Lauri Bowen-Vaccare: I am so very sorry. I've enjoyed reading stories about her, and seeing her beautiful face in my newsfeed. The last few months have, indeed, provided me with help for my own dogs and I think of Pepper every time we try one of your tricks. Thank you for sharing her with us - all of it. The good, the "bad," and everything in between - and for doing so honestly.

Kim Liz Ward: I'm so sorry, my friend. God bless you and Pepper. You gave her the best eight years, full of hope and love. You gave her a chance at life when no one else would. You both are angels. Love you both.

Missie Mattei: I'm in tears… your sharing has made the heroic love story of John and Pepper one close to my heart… a life changing Journey… I wish you both comfort and peace xo

Regina Stier: My thoughts and love are with you and Pepper. Words cannot express the thanks for all you have done for her and so many more by sharing her story. Run free Pepper…

Shelley Leong: Your story with her has been inspiring. Sending you love.

Julia Ferris: Blessings and love to Pepper and you. You have both been an inspiration in the dog lover's community.

Lesley Lynam: Thank you for sharing your journey together John, we share your loss and wish Pepper a smooth ride to the rainbow. She will see you again and the piece of your heart she takes with you leaves room … just in case another needs you.

Jenny Pavlovic: Thank you for your patience and willingness to work with her when she had no other options. You were lucky to find each other.

Ursula Hummel: My heart aches for you as you walk this last road with Pepper. I am so pleased that you both found each other and had such wonderful years together. Run fast, run far, run free, dear Pepper! And know that we'll all keep our eye out for John.

Sandy Modell: So sorry for your loss of Pepper.. Thanks for sharing her story. It was beautiful!

Cristine Dahl: Have been inspired by following your journey with Pepper and the lessons learned reach far beyond her time here. She leaves a legacy of compassion for both dogs and people. Thank you for sharing her with the world. We are better for it.

Hilary Lane: Thank you for sharing everything about your journey together over the years. I will miss that, but I know in my heart she was a very special dog and will remember your trials and happy times that you shared. Her loss and your videos bring me to tears. You and she were together as a team, although difficult at times, you made her life so much better.

Christy Hill: John, the shock after reading about your journey on FB for a while that it was her time. Their short time is everlasting love. How fortunate Pepper learned your love, some dogs never get that.

Ilene Keyes Isaacs: Rest peacefully sweet Pepper. You will know only respect and forever hold in your heart the incredible love your human had for you. And John, please hold in your heart the incredible impact you had on sweet Pepper's life and the lives of all of us the two of you have touched.

Linda D'Angelo Tack: So very sorry to hear about Pepper. I know how very much you both loved each other. So glad you saved her and am moved by the way you loved each other. Rest In Peace Pepper

Videos of Scenes Referenced in the Book
Available at www.pepperbecoming.com

1. "Jump" Pepper performing the first trick we learned together.
2. Snow! Pepper's first snow frolic after living in shelters for two years. My musical composition "Pepper" is the soundtrack.
3. Whale Eye! Pepper giving me a whale eye (sign of distress) and two quick snarls as I approach her while she has a bone.
4. Not Happy! Pepper erupting at the front door when she sees the mailman. Two weeks later, after learning a new cue, "Party time," she immediately runs from the door after hearing the cue.
5. Ding the Bell! Pepper taking her "Ding the Bell" trick outside, in the snow.
6. The Look!
7. The Olympics - Trying to prevent her from grumbling. The Portuguese Water Dog.
8. Pepper's Soul.
9. "This is coming to you live…"
10. The "untrainable" dog.
11. Ooops! Trainer fail and loving every minute of it.
12. Sniff-In-A-Bag.
13. "Come What May" The lullaby inspired by Pepper.
14. Over the Rainbow - A celebration of her life.

Made in the USA
Columbia, SC
17 August 2018